Pregnancy
and Child Care
for Healthy Living

Margaret Roberts

SPEARHEAD

Published by Spearhead
An imprint of New Africa Books (Pty) Ltd
99 Garfield Road
Kenilworth
7700
www.newafricabooks.co.za
info@newafricabooks.co.za

First edition 2003

ISBN 0-86486-551-1

Warning:
The content of this book is not intended as a substitute for consultation with a medical professional. Do not undertake any course of treatment without the advice of your doctor. The author and publishers take no responsibility for any illness or discomfort that may result from information contained in this book.

Managing editor: Anita van Zyl
Copy-editor: Kathleen Sutton
Cover photographs: Phyllis Green
Cover design: Peter Stuckey
Design and typesetting: Peter Stuckey
Printed and bound by Clyson Printers, 11th Avenue, Maitland

ontents

*I*ntroduction

Probably the most important time in your child's life is in the womb. Your health, and thus the health of your unborn baby, will form the foundation for his or her future – and what greater gift can we give our children than that of perfect health? When I was pregnant with my first child, my grandmother gave me this advice: 'Do all you can to be in perfect health. Eat wisely, drink wisely, rest wisely and think wisely, and create within you the picture of a perfect child – no matter be it boy or girl – a perfect, bonny, healthy child is all that counts.'

This, therefore, is what this little book is about. I hope to give you some ideas, borne of my own experience in carrying and bearing three children, to help you have a healthy baby and to keep your child that way in his or her first years in the world through using natural foods and herbs.

Before you begin, however, I must offer a word of caution. Always work with your doctor and never diagnose anything yourself. Ask your doctor's advice, keep him or her notified of what you are eating, how you are feeling and, once the baby is born, anything that worries you about yourself or your baby.

The recipes I give, the guidelines to healthy eating and the treatments for common everyday ailments in both mother and child are the results of long years of working with herbs and health-giving food. I offer no better advertisement than my own three children, Peter, Gail and Sandra, who are all healthy, vibrant individuals. I have them to thank for all the things they taught me and it is because of them that I am able to write this book. They suffered my experiments, my inexperience and my struggles to make them healthy beings. Peter's allergies and illnesses as a baby sparked off my interest in herbs and intensified my search for natural alternatives. His problems turned my thinking away from antibiotics and chemicals to natural medicines. He changed my outlook and set my feet on the path lined with herbs. I used herbs to soothe his cough, clear his nappy rash, calm his sleep and flavour his food. It was a frantic time, with fear and worry as my close companions. In and out of hospital, I took him to every doctor I knew and he baffled them all. Allergy tests showed dogs, grasses, horses and house dust as his greatest irritants. We lived on a farm – how ever did you get rid of those? Finally, a wise paediatrician suggested that I look with utmost care to his diet and I read up on herbs and experimented with all I could and eventually emerged with a healthy son, and the comfort of much knowledge. My two daughters reaped the benefits of my studies, and it is with a thankful heart that I share with you my children's attainment of health and wellbeing.

In 1989 when I wrote the original series of small herb books that included a herbal approach to pregnancy and child care, I wanted the books to be 'user-friendly', so that a busy young mother could quickly refer to them and could easily apply the recipes and advice given. Since then we have welcomed two more little babies into our family, Tom and Samantha, and I found myself constantly thinking of even easier ways to help the young mother. As this book goes to print, my youngest daughter Sandra's pregnancy with her first child has added new dimensions to the pregnancy chapter. What an exciting time!

So this updated book includes new recipes and new information with the Biochemic Tissue Salts. No mother should be without my little book *Tissue Salts for Healthy Living*, published by Spearhead. I was pregnant with my second baby when I started to use the easily and inexpensively obtainable Tissue Salts (available at most chemists across the world). I use Natura Tissue Salts manufactured by Homeopathic Laboratory in Hazelwood, Pretoria, as I find their tablets easiest to use.

A healthy diet for both mother and child is the foundation on which all else depends. I am more and more anxious that fast foods warmed in microwaves are the norm, and judging from the modern problems of hyperactivity and lack of concentration and frazzled parents and teachers, I've put together a section that will help.

'Keeping it natural' helps to build health, without resorting to preservatives, colourants, stabilisers, flavour enhancers, permitted flavours, etc. Learn to read the labels. It doesn't take much more time making a substantial stew or soup or meat loaf, and I usually make enough for two meals so that I can warm up the second half for the next day, but never in a microwave. The safer and easier way is to warm it, well covered, in the oven, or over a pot of boiling water in a smaller pot, or stir gently on the stove until it is warmed through.

It's also easy to make natural flavourings using herbs and spices rather than using monosodium glutamate (MSG) flavourings, and to lighten up on both the salt and sugar. These will not only build up health, but also minimise those temper tantrums and irritability.

This is a fabulous journey you are now beginning. Give it all your attention – your 'alert button' needs to be set permanently on 'ON'. My grandmother wisely said: 'Sweets are dangerous', and we grew up with only one on a Sunday, and then not every Sunday. Bringing my children up on a farm they didn't have access to the café or the corner shop, but I became adept at making dried fruit mixes and tasty treats with honey and sunflower seeds, and when they were given sweets by visitors and friends I always tried to ration them.

And that is what this little book is all about – building up healthy little people and a strong and healthy and happy Mom.

Enjoy!

My thanks go to my publishers for giving this little book a new life, to the clinic sisters across the country who teach the new mothers from these pages and to the young mothers who have so enthusiastically given me such positive feedback!

Conversion tables

Volume

ml to Teaspoons	ml to Tablespoons	ml to Cups	ml to Pints
1 ml = ¼ tsp	12,5 ml = 1 tbsp	60 ml = ¼ cup	570 ml = 1 pt
2 ml = ½ tsp	25 ml = 2 tbsp	80ml = ⅓ cup	1,1 l = 2 pts
5 ml = 1 tsp	37,5 ml = 3 tbsp	125 ml = ½ cup	1,7 l = 3 pts
10 ml = 2 tsp	50 ml = 4 tbsp	180 ml = ¾ cup	2,3 l = 4 pts
15 ml = 3 tsp		250 ml = 1 cup	
20 ml = 4 tsp		500 ml = 2 cups	
		750 ml = 3 cups	
		1 litre = 4 cups	

Mass

Grams to Ounces	g/kg to Pounds
30 g = 1 oz	450 g = 1 lb
60 g = 2 oz	900 g = 2 lb
125 g = 4 oz	1,4 kg = 3 lb
250 g = 8 oz	1,8 kg = 4 lb
	2,3 kg = 5 lb

Oven temperatures	Celsius (°C)	Fahrenheit (ºF)
Very cool	100 – 120	210 – 250
Cool	130 – 160	270 – 320
Moderate	170 – 180	340 – 360
Moderately hot	190 – 210	370 – 410
Hot	220 – 240	430 – 460
Very hot	250 +	480 +

Congratulations – you're pregnant!

The ancient Greeks took particular care of their child-bearing women and perhaps we could take a few lessons from their philosophy today. A few months before conception, women were taken to a special place of tranquillity. Here their diets were watched over by trained 'nurses' and they listened to beautiful music, were offered only pure foods and drank fresh spring water and goat's milk. Their husbands could visit them constantly but the women remained in the peaceful environment (no interfering mothers-in-law, family or friends!). Then, once they were pregnant, they spent the next nine months there, bathing in the natural pools in those beautiful surroundings, walking in the gardens that were exquisitely laid out with statues, fountains and fragrant flowers. They continued their diet of natural foods and drinks, while their nurses soothed their backs and stretching bodies with fragrant oils. No harsh sounds or words or anxieties were allowed to disturb them. What an enchanting time to allow one's baby to grow within those unstressed bodies, but how impractical for today's woman! There are few of us who could lay claim to that sort of time, or are able to escape life's daily stresses, or indeed afford such luxury.

So often a pregnancy is not even planned and no time is available to think about diet or a change in lifestyle. Still – better late than never! As soon as you know that you are pregnant, for the sake of your own health and that of the life now within you, the following important steps should be taken.

1

Avoid:

- all refined, processed, treated, tinned, stabilised, 'junk' foods
- all alcohol
- all tranquillisers, aspirin, pep-pills, sleeping pills etc. (Discuss any medication you may be on with your doctor.)
- fad dieting
- stimulants, e.g. caffeine-rich beverages, artificial creamers in teas, instant coffee
- curries, chutneys and condiments. The hot spicy flavourings will increase the chances of heartburn and digestive discomfort
- watching TV, being near microwave ovens and using microwaves, cell phones and computers.

Get your thoughts around 'electro-magnetic pollution'. Without thinking we expose ourselves to so much of it. We sit long hours in front of the TV and computers, filling our bodies with radiation, and wonder why we have no energy and feel so tired.

There are several things that can help. Eat two apples every day. The pectin in the apples will help to clear the irradiation, but peel them first to get rid of the pesticides that are soaked into the skin, or source some organically grown apples. And don't keep the apples anywhere near the computer or TV. Take kelp tablets daily to help clear irradiation – follow the directions on the box and be sure to discuss this with your doctor first to see if he or she would like you to take it during your pregnancy and if you're breastfeeding.

Use sea salt in the bath. Tie a good handful of sea salt in a face cloth and wet it thoroughly with warm water. Stand in the bath and use strong brisk strokes away from the heart to cleanse away the day's pollution. (I often tied in a few fresh lavender or rose-scented geranium leaves.) Keep dipping the salted cloth into the hot water and rub out all the day's accumulation from the neck downwards, from chest to fingertips, from thigh to ankle, and do this until the salt dissolves. Then lie back in the bath and feel the refreshing tingle.

Add another handful of salt to the water and massage your thighs and buttocks (to break down cellulite) and over your back to release tension, then use soap and wash gently all over. You'll emerge refreshed but relaxed, and your skin will feel great.

Once you've dried off in the biggest, softest towel you can find, lavish some soothing body lotion or cream all over, giving extra attention to breasts and nipples and over the tummy and all over the feet. Massage in well.

Extra moisturising body cream

Easy to make and exquisitely soothing, this is one of the basic body creams I have found to be the best over the years, and it's safe for baby too.

In a double boiler, warm 1 tub good aqueous cream with 1 cup finely chopped fresh comfrey leaves, and 1 cup fresh rose petals (unsprayed roses only), and 1 cup calendula petals. (Use ½ cup dried petals if calendula, which only grows in the winter months, is unavailable – but be sure to grow it every winter to make this precious cream.)

Add ½ cup almond oil and simmer gently. Stir well every now and then and simmer for 20 minutes. Remove from the heat and strain. Discard the herbs and add 3 teaspoons of vitamin E oil and ½–1 teaspoon of pure rose essential oil (bought from the chemist). Mix well. Ladle into a sterilised jar and keep in the bathroom and apply after the bath. It will soothe and soften the skin.

The computer plant of the future

Sacred or Holy Basil. Also known as Tulsi (*Ocimum sanctum*)
This is one of the world's most incredible plants and your nursery will order it for you as part of the Margaret Roberts Malanseuns Herb Collection. It is a perennial basil and is richly and spicily fragrant, predominantly with a clove-like scent. You can grow it in a pot as large as is comfortable to carry for it has to be moved out of the room where the computer is every three days and placed in the sun and watered well, and every month given a little seaweed or natural fertiliser.

Spray the leaves with a plant mister every day, don't let it dry out inside. Place it near a window and the whole room will feel fresh and alive. This precious plant absorbs electro-magnetic pollution, and gives off such amazingly healing oils that the whole area benefits. An ancient healing herb that was much revered and

3

respected, this could be our lifesaver of the future. The leaves can be used in the bath and for teas to heal all sorts of ailments, but use only the ones growing in the garden – not the plants that have been clearing the radiation indoors.

Grow several sacred basil plants in containers so that you can swop them around, bringing some indoors and keeping the others outside in full sun, well watered and fed.

Diet

Include in your diet:
- natural, unrefined foods
- wholewheat meal and bran in homemade bread (learn to bake your own)
- raisins, dates and honey if you have a sweet tooth, rather than sweets and chocolates
- plenty of fresh fruit and vegetables
- increased fluids in the form of mild herb teas, pure, fresh water and milk
- plain yoghurt and buttermilk
- vitamins. Ask your doctor to advise you on increasing your vitamin supplements; vitamin C and vitamin B complex are essential.
- proteins (meat, fish, poultry, milk, eggs, nuts, butter, cheese, beans, specially broadbeans and butterbeans, black-eyed peas, lentils and chickpeas).

Basic menu for healthy eating in pregnancy

Breakfast

- *Fruit* – one portion of any of the following: pawpaw (excellent to keep the stomach working well), mango, orange (with a little of the white rind), grapefruit, peach, apple, grape, apricots, figs, strawberries, pears, litchis, plums.
- *Yoghurt* – about half a cup.
- One helping of homemade *muesli*, with yoghurt and hot or cold milk.

4

To make your own muesli

This is enough for eight servings.
4 cups oats – non-instant kind
1–2 cups chopped pecan nuts and almonds
1 cup sultanas
1 cup sunflower seeds
1–2 cups chopped mixed dried fruit, e.g. figs, apricots, pears, apple
    rings, prunes
1 cup digestive bran

Mix everything together well. Store in a sealed container in the fridge.
Serve with plain yoghurt and warm milk. Don't sweeten it – there is a
lot of natural sugar in the fruit.

- Slice of wholewheat toast, with a little honey, Marmite or cream cheese.
- Herb tea – lemon balm, mint or peppermint all make a delicious start to the day. To make a herb tea use a quarter cup fresh herbs, pour over this one cup boiling water, stand for five minutes, then strain. Sweeten to taste with a little honey, or add a squeeze of lemon juice.

Mid-morning

- A cup of buttermilk or plain unsweetened yoghurt or a cup of herb tea, e.g. ginger, mint, melissa, etc.
- A glass of whole milk or a piece of fresh fruit. (Add a little fresh wheatgerm, about ten m*l* daily, to your milk.)

Lunch

- A green salad – include, for example, lettuce, spinach, beetroot tops or dandelion greens. Top with a health salad dressing: mix a quarter cup oil, freshly squeezed lemon juice and 250 m*l* honey in a screw-top jar. Seal and shake well. Add one to two teaspoons of either chopped thyme, mint, sage, oregano or tarragon.

Or

5

Steamed vegetables, seasoned with lemon juice and a light sprinkling of thyme or marjoram or tarragon and a sprinkle of grated cheese – mozzarella or sweet milk.

Or

Baked potato, split open and with a little cream or cottage cheese, mixed with chopped chives or parsley, pushed into it.
- For dessert, fresh whole or mashed fruit, with or without a little yoghurt on top.
- A glass of fresh milk if no yoghurt is eaten.

Mid-afternoon

- Freshly squeezed fruit juice, fruit shake or herb tea.

Fruit shake

In a liquidiser whirl ½ cup milk with 1 banana, 5 almonds, 1 apple, peeled and quartered, or 1 pear, peeled and quartered, with a sprinkle of cinnamon. Substitute strawberries or peaches or nectarines, etc., whatever fruit is in season.

Dinner

- Vegetable soup.

Homemade vegetable soup

Serves ten plus.
This is my best-loved, most fabulous stand-by soup I never get tired of, and I also make it with a whole chicken for supper for the entire family.

Soak 1 cup of butter beans overnight.
In a large pot brown 3 large chopped onions in a little olive oil.
Add 2 cups chopped celery and stirfry with 3 cups chopped tomatoes.
Add 2 cups chopped green pepper.
Then add 3 cups grated carrot, 2 cups grated pumpkin, 2 cups grated sweet potato.

Now add 1 litre stock and stir.
Add 1 cup pearl barley, 1 cup lentils and 1 cup split peas and the drained butter beans.
Add 2–4 teaspoons salt, 1 teaspoon cayenne pepper, 3-4 teaspoons Marmite (or a whole small chicken).
Add the juice of 2 lemons and 2 litres of water, stir and simmer for 2 hours. Top up with more water when needed.

I add a little thyme, chopped basil and borage as well and, served with crusty bread, this is a nourishing healthy meal. I still serve it all through the winter and every chance I get.

- Poached or boiled egg with wholewheat bread and cottage cheese.

Or

- Chicken or beef or fish with steamed vegetables or salad with sprouts.
- Fresh fruit
- A glass of milk, warmed and sweetened with a little honey, just before bedtime, or one cup of chamomile tea or mint tea. I found peppermint the best: one thumb-length sprig to one cup boiling water, stand five minutes, then strain and sip slowly. Also melissa tea and lemon thyme are very comforting.

Biochemic Tissue Salts

This will astonish you – Biochemic Tissue Salts have been my life-saver through all my pregnancies.

I used mainly Ferrum Phos. No. 4, Kali. Mur. No. 5, Nat. Phos. No. 10 and Nat. Sulph. No. 11.

I took 5 and 10, then took 4 and 11. I lived on them, taking two of each – sucked under the tongue – frequently, sometimes ten times a day. After a week or so I needed less and less. Read up all about them in *Tissue Salts for Healthy Living*, published by Spearhead.

7

Vitamins

During pregnancy and while you are breastfeeding your baby, extra vitamins are essential if you want to maintain peak health for both of you. Consult your doctor here; he or she will probably recommend a supplement of vitamin B complex and vitamin E. Your vitamin intake needs to be carefully balanced in these important months. Be warned though – too much is as bad as too little, so do take your doctor's advice.

If you are able to plan ahead, vitamin E can be used for some months before pregnancy. It helps keep the body in shape as it is known to firm up muscle tone. It is also known to firm up sagging breasts and stomach muscles after the baby is born, as well as varicosities. Wheatgerm and wheatgerm oil are good sources of vitamin E and an easy and healthy way of increasing its intake in your diet. Make sure to buy a reputable brand and see that it is fresh. Keep it in the fridge once you have started using it.

Vitamin C fights infections, keeps skin and muscle tone in tip-top condition and, in fact, is essential to one's wellbeing, especially during the winter months. Vitamin C will actually give you an energy boost – 500 mg at midday will see you into your evening activities if you feel yourself flagging. Do not take vitamin C after 4 p.m. however.

These two vitamins are freely available on the market. Between your chemist and your doctor work out a suitable programme for yourself.

Constipation

Constipation can become a very real problem for the expectant mother, but it is a problem which can so easily be sorted out through correct eating. It is essential that you have at least one bowel movement a day. Toxins and waste need to be cleansed from your system in order to keep blood and body fluids moving and bringing nourishment to your unborn child. Prevent constipation by:
• drinking water, at least four glasses a day. It should be fresh and pure, without juice or flavouring of any kind.

- including roughage in your diet, e.g. wholewheat bread, bran, breakfast muesli.
- eating fruit. Pawpaw, prunes soaked overnight in water, and grapes all have laxative properties.
- including oil in the diet. Sunflower or maize oil are easiest to digest. Use them in stirfry dishes and in salad dressings.

Try Margaret Roberts Herbal Remedies "Intestinal Cleanser" manufactured by Fithealth. It should be available from your chemist.

If constipation is already a problem for you, try the following recipe:

2 tablespoons each of:
digestive bran
sunflower oil
skimmed milk powder

Mix together and add to your breakfast muesli, porridge, mashed fruit or yoghurt. This recipe has proved to be infallible. Take it each morning until your bowel movements are easy and regular again. If you are chronically constipated, consult your doctor immediately. Avoid any harsh laxatives during pregnancy.

Exercise

Pregnancy is an important period to keep the body trim, supple and vigorous. Antenatal classes should be a time of pleasure for expectant mothers. Encourage your baby's father to come along too and get fit alongside you. It will give him a chance of getting to know the changes your body is undergoing and to appreciate any aches and pains you may experience. This is a good opportunity for couples to exercise together and to support each other.

Antenatal classes should include back exercises, pelvic floor exercises (to strengthen those muscles used in labour) and, most important, breathing exercises. A good instructor will use rhythm and music and by the end of the class the mothers-to-be will emerge flushed and radiant, circulation moving and stiffness gone.

These are joyful classes and I urge you to attend them. Find out about them from your doctor, hospital or clinic, or join a gym that offers such classes. Take care, though, that you have a qualified person to teach you, for this is a crucial time in your life and that of your baby, and wrong exercising can do untold damage. Do the exercises at home too, particularly the breathing ones. These will keep your lungs strong and help you when you go into labour. As a physiotherapist I gave both ante- and post-natal classes and witnessed visible changes in every mother. This is important! Do it!

Relaxation

Relaxation is as important as exercise during pregnancy. A midday rest is ideal, but as this blissful activity is often not possible, catnaps or just moments of putting your feet up and doing some deep-breathing exercises every now and then will have to suffice. If you can manage a midday lie-down, try lying in the following position. (During all three of my pregnancies I found this to be the most comfortable position of all and, as the baby grew, almost the only really peaceful way of lying down.)

Turn on your side, placing your head on a not-too-high pillow. Turn the upper shoulder towards the pillow, arm bent and hand tucked beneath it. Twist the hips so that the upper bent leg rests on another pillow. The leg underneath should be straight or slightly flexed. The arm underneath should be straight too. The pelvis and abdomen are thus supported on the bed and the weight is lifted.

You will find that the baby enjoys this position too; mine kicked vigorously the minute I wanted to sleep, but I found it so comfortable I didn't mind! Practise in the early months to get used to resting this way so that with the increased weight you will find it easy to relax into. Twenty minutes lying comfortably on your bed, supported by pillows and breathing deeply, will help you unwind.

I found, too, that quiet, restful music had a calming effect on both myself and the baby. (I also played gentle music while I breastfed in a comfortable armchair and I found my babies had hardly any wind.) Try to avoid all loud, jarring sounds and heavy beats. Believe it or not, peaceful sounds make peaceful babies, and quiet classical music while your baby is in the womb will soothe your child all his life.

Sleep

Sleep during pregnancy is vital for both you and the unborn baby. Make the most of it – it is probably the last chance you will have for an undisturbed eight hours for quite some time! In my very first pregnancy I created the 'peace pillow' and I found that I slept well and always woke with a clear head. This is a small pillow filled with calming herbs such as lavender, mint, scented geranium or rose petals. It is light and easy to carry about with you and it also soothes aching backs or stiff necks. Twenty-five years later I still advocate the use of a peace pillow, pregnant or not, for a restful sleep. In fact I am never without one. It is easy and pleasureable to make:

Peace pillow

Inner lining: Take a piece of polyester cotton, 30 cm x 20 cm, and sew it up into a rectangle, leaving a 12 cm opening along one side. I sew a double row of stitches as this will keep the finer herbs from escaping.
Cover: Make the cover 1 cm bigger all the way round, with a flap of 8 cm. Choose a pretty print in a soft voile or polyester cotton. Use a fabric that does not crease and will wash easily. Make it up as you would a pillowcase and edge with lace.

Filling: Half fill your pillow with soft foam chips (usually about 6 cups of foam, depending on how firm you like it). Meanwhile lay your herbs out to dry. Place them on a newspaper in the shade, using enough herbs to make two cups of leaves and flowers. The following filling is a beautifully fragrant one:

2 cups scented geranium leaves
3 cups rose petals
1 cup peppermint leaves
2 cups lavender leaves and flowers
1 cup minced dried lemon peel and pips
2 sticks cinnamon, broken into small pieces
½ cup whole cloves
lavender oil

Mix dry ingredients and add a few drops of oil. Store in a tightly sealed crock or jar. Shake daily. After ten days add a little more oil until you are satisfied with the fragrance. Store for another week, then turn in the foam chips and mix well.

Stuff the inner case of your pillow with this fragrant mixture and sew up the opening. Place it inside your outer pillowcase and enjoy the pillow's beautiful comfort and scent. When the aroma starts to fade, turn the contents out into the crock again, add a few drops of lavender oil, shake daily for two days, then return the mixture to your pillow. Add a little fresh lavender if you like.

I have kept one of my babies' tiny lawn pillowcases for years. After a particularly hard day, when I've been too tense or rushed, I go into the garden in the cool of the evening and pick a bunch of leaves from my rose-scented geranium and some lavender sprigs. Sometimes a little lemon verbena goes in too. I strip these leaves from their twigs and push them into the pillowcase. I bruise the soft bundle a little and tuck it behind or beside my big pillow. I always sleep soundly and wake much refreshed – what better sleeping pill! The leaves keep for two or three days, after which I shake them out onto newspaper and dry them for adding to pot-pourris.

Another way of unwinding and relaxing after a hard day is to pick a bunch of fresh scented geranium leaves, lavender leaves and flowers, and mint. Bruise them slightly and place them in a big bowl next to your bed. You will find that you sleep very well that night.

Bathing

Very few things can beat a warm bath for relaxing and unwinding. Living in a very hot part of the country when I was pregnant, I found I sometimes needed to bathe both morning and evening during the summer, or at least freshen up with a brisk, lukewarm shower. At the end of the day, however, a soak in a herb-scented bath is the easiest way of ensuring a good night's rest.

Bath herbs can be varied: lemon balm (melissa), the lavenders, the scented geraniums, the mints, sage, rose petals, calendula, violets (leaves and flowers), oatmeal (for itchy skin), thyme, jasmine or honeysuckle flowers will all restore and revive. For further herbal baths, see *Herbs for Health and Beauty* in the Margaret Roberts Herb Series.

Skin

During pregnancy your skin needs special care. Some women get away without any of those silvery lines over the abdomen, hips, buttocks and breasts which pregnancy causes. There are some precautions you can take to avoid them. For a start, the increased intake of vitamin C aids the elasticity of the tissues. During my own pregnancies I took 1 000 mg a day and I never had a mark.

Comfrey cream with vitamin E can be rubbed into the skin every evening after your bath to prevent stretchmarks. The all-purpose massage oil is also effective, and wheatgerm oil used as a massage oil is also excellent. For three days infuse a sprig of rosemary in it for extra healing over taut skin.

All-purpose massage oil

1 sprig rosemary
1 sprig chamomile leaves and flowers
medicinal olive oil (available at chemists)
vitamin E capsules
1 tablespoon almond oil
1 teaspoon rose geranium essential oil

Infuse the rosemary and chamomile in the bottle of olive oil for three or four days. Strain through muslin or a fine sieve and, to a 500 g-bottle, add four vitamin E capsules (pierce the soft capsule and squeeze out the contents), 1 tablespoon almond oil and the rose geranium essential oil. Put through a blender and massage the resulting oil into the skin, a little at a time. This is also a wonderful massage for cuticles and cracked skin around heels and toes, as well as rough patches on knees and elbows.

Home-made comfrey cream with vitamin E

In a double boiler melt 1 cup good aqueous cream and 1 cup an-hydrous lanolin, bought from your chemist. Simmer these together in the double boiler. Add 3 teaspoons vitamin E oil and ½ cup almond oil and, when all four are well combined, add 1 cup chopped comfrey leaves. Simmer for 20 minutes, then strain through a fine sieve and ladle into a sterilised jar with a good tight lid. Massage the cream into the stomach and breasts during pregnancy, as well as post-natally.

13

This cream is also excellent for toughening the nipples in preparation for breastfeeding. It will soothe cracked, sore nipples too. Remember, though, to wash nipples thoroughly with warm, soapy water before each feed.

Morning sickness

Some fortunate women breeze through the early months of pregnancy without even feeling queasy, while others battle constantly with nausea and morning sickness. If at all possible, however, I would strongly advise you never to take medicines and treatments for morning sickness as these first weeks are critical in the life of that tiny foetus inside you and so much can harm it. Try rather to use natural means and treatments and try to remember that at the very most morning sickness will only last three months.

Tissue Salts: No. 4, No. 5, No. 10, No. 11. Suck two of each frequently.

Dr Bach's Rescue Remedy

This 'wonder drop' contains a Harley Street specialist's five herbs, all of them anti-shock. A few drops on the tongue at frequent intervals (every few minutes if necessary) will quickly ease the nausea. Rescue Remedy is available at health stores and some pharmacies.

Lemon juice

A little fresh lemon juice squeezed into a glass of cold water and sipped frequently will ease the symptoms of morning sickness. If yours is a winter pregnancy, lemon juice in hot water is comforting and as effective. In summer, add a bit of ice.

Herb teas

Never put milk into herb teas, and usually one or two cups of a specific herb per day is enough but you can drink different herb teas all through the day.

Standard brew

A number of herbs are wonderfully effective in gently and quickly treating a variety of ailments. Pour 1 cup of boiling water over ¼ cup of fresh herbs. Leave it to stand for 4–5 minutes. Strain, sweeten with a touch of honey if liked, add a squeeze of lemon juice if liked, and sip slowly.

Favourite herb teas are:

- *Lemon Balm* (melissa) for all sorts of digestive disturbances including colic, heartburn, hiccoughs, bloatedness and flatulence.
- *Ginger* – thin slices of the root will help colds, coughs, flu, morning sickness and nausea.
- *Rose-scented geranium* will calm, soothe and unwind and is a wonderful sleepy time tea.
- *Chamomile flowers* – another unwinding herb and sleep inducer. Calming and soothing.
- *Lemongrass* – an energy giving tea, refreshing and delicious.
- *The mints* – all are digestive and soothing to the whole digestive system. Peppermint also helps clarity of thought, as well as easing nausea, colic and stomach cramps.

Fight the heat

For the mother-to-be a heat wave can be wearying, and here I watch Sandra carefully, as her baby is due in the hottest part of the mid-summer. Here are some 'heat-busters' – natural ways of safely soothing heat rash and the discomfort of perspiration and sticky heat in every situation.

Rule number one

I am always wary of fans and air-conditioners. If the heat is too unbearable without air-conditioning, then a short while in an air-conditioned room can be a lifesaver. See how you feel – you want to avoid being chilled and then exposed to that engulfing wave of heat that threatens to floor us as we step out into it. So turn the air-conditioning to low and keep a fan slowly moving the air upwards. Remember hot air rises – so position the fan so that it swirls the air up and not directly onto you.

Rule number two

Make up the bed with a tightly tucked-in percale sheet. Invest in a few percale or finely woven pure cotton sheets and pillowcases, or better still, a fine linen sheet and, if you're lucky, a linen pillowcase or two. You won't believe the smooth coolness. Forget the creases, this is the way to keep the body cool and stressless, as the cotton and linen absorbs the sticky heat moisture, the perspiration, and keeps the skin fresh.

Let the bed be your sanctuary on a hot afternoon. Spray, lightly, a refreshing linen spray over the sheet. You'll be surprised at the pleasure it will give you.

Making the linen spray

Simmer 10 fully open fragrant roses (unsprayed of course) in 2 litres of water with 10 cloves and a stick of cinnamon, and 2 or 3 twists of finely pared lemon peel. If you don't have roses, use 3 or 4 cups of either fresh lemon verbena leaves or rose-scented geranium leaves, and add the cloves and the cinnamon and the lemon peel. Simmer with the lid half on for 15 minutes. Then cool and strain. Pour into a spritz bottle – the sort you buy at a nursery for misting plants. Add 4–8 drops of rose essential oil and shake up well. Stand a short distance from the bed and lightly spray the fine mist in arcs over the bed, shaking often. It will immediately cool the air and the sheet as well. Keep the excess in the fridge. This fragrant mist is safe to spray on your arms and legs and feet and all around you. Keep shaking it as you spray as oil and water don't mix and you need to disperse the precious essential oils.

16

When I was pregnant with my middle child, I survived an excep-
tionally hot summer by making my rose-water spray just by
boiling up fresh roses – no spices, no peel, no essential oil – and
I have always come to associate the glorious smell of rose-water
with being pregnant in a heat wave and feeling the calm refreshing
comfort rose-water gives, as well as softening, soothing and pam-
pering the skin. Remember, even just plain water in a mister sprayed
frequently all over yourself, head to toe, will revive you amazingly.

Rule number three

Keep a thermos flask of iced water near at hand for frequent sips.
Squeeze half a lemon into a small jug of iced water and add at least
2 cups of crushed ice. Gently pour into a thermos flask (watch how
you fill it as ice can crack the fragile glass inside of the flask). Have
a glass handy and pour a small quantity at a time and keep a bottle
of Tissue Salt No. 9 – Nat. Mur. – at the bedside. It helps to break
the heat, control the perspiration and quench the thirst, and with
No. 4 – Ferrum Phos. – and No. 8 – Mag. Phos. – will normalise the
body temperature and help you to relax. Let one tablet of each dis-
solve under the tongue every couple of hours or so.

Rule number four

Fill a basin of cold water and every now and then immerse the
hands and forearms up over the elbows in it for one minute. I add a
couple of sprigs of lavender to this, leaves and all, and allow my
hands and arms to drip dry. This small effort makes a world of difference. Splash the face and neck too, and let everything drip dry.

Rule number five

Plan your day. Do all the chores early on in the day. Sort out the
evening meal for the rest of the family. Plan things like cold chicken
or cold roast beef and salads and fruit salad for dinner and cook the
chicken or the roast first thing in the morning. Go to the shops as
soon as they open while the air is still cool and you'll avoid the

rush and flurry of the crowds and you'll enjoy the peacefulness of early shopping. I made the daily bread at 5 a.m. every morning, and then could relax with a cool breakfast of chilled fruit and yoghurt and toast after everyone had bustled out for the day. It was my lifesaver – a mere reorganisation of my heat-heavy time. Concentrate on cool foods, lots of iced watermelon, lots of chilled salads, lots of iced soups and reconsider juicing.

Often the pregnant mother doesn't feel hungry – it's too hot to eat, it's too much effort, and there is a heat-weariness you're unable to explain. Keep the juicer set up and ready to go. Toss in a quartered peeled carrot or two or three, a quartered peeled raw beetroot or two, three sticks of celery, a quartered peeled apple, a handful of parsley and a squeeze of lemon juice. Have a glass ready to catch the juice and drink it slowly and immediately – don't let it discolour or stand.

Other juicy energisers

1. 1/2 spanspek melon, diced and chilled
   1/2 green melon, diced and chilled
   1 tablespoon grated fresh ginger
   (This is a favourite late summer afternoon reviver.)
2. 2 peeled peaches, halved
   1 peeled banana, sliced
   1 peeled apple, quartered
3. 1 bunch washed grapes
   1 apple, peeled and quartered
   1 carrot, peeled and diced
4. 1/2 pineapple, peeled and chunked
   2 carrots, peeled and diced
   2 sticks celery, diced
5. 2 slices of peeled watermelon, chilled
   2 sprigs of mint
6. 2 ripe tomatoes, quartered
   1 green pepper, sliced and de-seeded
   handful of fresh parsley
   2 sticks celery

You'll soon find your favourites and tasty combinations will become an art. Listen to your own body's desires – maybe nectarines and grapes are all you want one day, and the next maybe it's strawberries with apricots, and the next oranges with spearmint, and the next ruby grapefruit with pears. You choose. You'll be thrilled by the ease of juicing and the small amount of effort required. Cheers! Drink up!

The bath

This is one of the real lifesavers. The actual relaxation in lukewarm water or, on a scorcher of a day, tepid or cold water, is the most effective way of cooling down. Some mothers-to-be find the huge effort of getting into and out of a bath uncomfortable. So give yourself the pleasure of the shower, it's incredible the difference that it makes. It's also worth getting someone to rig up an outdoor shower for you – even a hosepipe with a nozzle that can be attached to the wall or a fence or an arch with a smooth paving slab underneath it. The hosepipe heats up the water, so let it run a little first so as not to burn yourself! Then, and here is the secret, once you're wet, step out of the shower and take a wet face cloth, heap in it a cup, or a cup and a half, of coarse sea salt and add a sprig of mint such as peppermint, or Eau-de-Cologne mint, or pineapple mint, or a small bunch of lavender, or some thinly pared lemon peel, or a few rose geranium leaves, or some lemon verbena leaves, or some fresh and fragrant and non-sprayed rose petals. Tie everything up in the wet face cloth and soak it in the water and then with a sweeping movement gently wash away the fatigue and the heat exhaustion. Then step into the bath or under the shower, and massage the almost dissolved salt bag all over your body. When you step out and dry off, you'll feel as though you've had a swim in the sea.

Dressing for 'coolth'

Living as I do in a very hot area of the country with summer temperatures usually hovering between 33 °C and 35 °C, sometimes 36 °C, I have learned that white and light is the coolest colour to wear, without a doubt. Make yourself a soft, full loose dress – full so you won't need a petticoat, mid-calf length so you are not anxious about showing a bit of thigh or a glimpse of a leg, because everything feels expanded at this stage, and you want to feel comfortable after all. Gather or pleat the top of the dress into a pretty sleeveless yoke, and choose fine cotton or the coolest silky soft fabric. To test the fabric before buying it, wrap it around your hand and leave it for a minute. If it 'breathes', your hand will be cool, if it is synthetically unbreathing and your hand feels hot and sticky, you'll fry in it. Be careful of the fabric you choose – it needs to be light, soft and white or the palest of pastels, and easily washable. I made a wonderful maternity dress out of a percale sheet in palest shell pink and literally lived in it in the hot mid-summer months. I washed it every night and wore it gratefully the next day, and stayed cool and fresh all day. Even after I had the baby I found myself wearing it at the end of the hot summer just to keep my cool! This dress will become your lifeline. Forget the jeans, the mini and the shorts, nothing beats the coolness of a soft full tent!

Heat rash cream – that is safe for baby too

Use this comforting cream to smooth into hot itchy areas:
Pick 4 to 6 fresh elder flower heads, enough to equal 1 cup – elder trees bloom in summer and the exquisite white lacy flowers can be dried in the shade on newspaper and stored in a screw-top glass jar for winter use. Or if you don't have elder flowers, use 1 cup of fresh pennywort leaves – *Centella asiatica* – one of the world's most effective skin herbs that no garden should be without and it grows as easily in the sun as it does in light shade and makes a beautifully even and attractive ground cover. In a double boiler add 1 cup of good aqueous cream. (Buy the best one available – it's a little more expensive than the run of the mill aqueous creams.) Add the chopped fresh leaves or the elder flowers, add 10 cloves and simmer over the boiling water for 20 minutes, then strain, cool and stir in 2 teaspoons of vitamin E oil. Store in a sterilised jar and use lavishly, specially along the pantylines and in the groin.

A good rule to remember is to always test a little cream on the inside of the wrist first. Rub it in and then leave it for two to three minutes. Should it become itchy and red, rinse off with cold water to which a little apple cider vinegar has been added and pat dry. Test on baby too, to make sure.

Aqueous cream is a safe cream. Discuss it with your chemist first if you have any doubts. I have tried every aqueous cream on the market to date and never have had a bad reaction even from the really cheap ones, and this is why I use it confidently as a base for all my home-made creams.

Talc powder

Never underestimate the comfort of talc powder – from cooling hot sticky feet to under-arm refreshing, it's pure pleasure to the mother-to-be, but be sure never to inhale the fine particles – it's bad for the lungs. For this reason, and for the baby, start making your own 'safe' talc – and it's easy.

1 cup corn flour
1/2 cup rice flour
1 1/2 cups lavender flowers (Use only the Margaret Roberts Lavandula intermedia here) – strip the tiny flowers off their stems and spread on a tray and roll with a rolling pin – enough to give you 1 1/2 cups of flowers.

Stir the corn flour and the rice flour together. Spoon the mixture into a fine sieve and sift it into a flat glass dish that has been spread with lavender flowers. Mix in the lavender flowers gently with your washed fingers. Then cover with cling film. The rolling pin will have released the lavender oil so that it gives its fragrance off to the corn flour mixture. Keep well sealed in the glass dish for a week.

Give it a daily gentle shake to disperse the lavender flowers. Then finally sieve out the lavender flowers and discard. Shake the sieve well to get every little bit of fragrant talc off them – I do this over a piece of clean paper and carefully funnel the talc into a sterilised bottle with a lid that has holes pierced in it, or funnel it into an old well-washed talc dispenser.

Although I prefer glass as a container, I have to agree plastic, well-washed, is a safer dispenser in the bathroom as talc is slippery, so the glass container needs to be very carefully handled. Be on the lookout for plastic talc dispensers to store your home-made talc. This natural talc is far safer for the baby too – so make a good batch now and enjoy its immediate soothing, cooling effect.

Winter warming

During the winter my antenatal classes were a source of constant laughter when the mothers-to-be arrived wrapped in blankets and duvets and voluminous coats and boots and scarves. Some mothers-to-be claimed the baby took all the heat from their bodies, while others claimed all the circulation had forgotten to go to hands and feet – it was so busy going to the baby! So, together we formulated some warming tactics and *exercise* was one of them. After the two-hour session they all emerged warm and flushed and sparkling and discarded the coats and the blankets!

Rule number one

Choose simple, easy-to-do exercises that don't make you uncomfortable if you can't join an antenatal class, and do them religiously – it will get the circulation moving. Don't neglect the daily walk, even if it's bitterly cold outside – put on the gloves and the scarf and the anorak and sturdy boots, and brave the cold. Wait for the midday warmth to clear the frost and stride it out. You'll return invigorated, flushed and warm! Make exercise the first warming rule.

Rule number two

Warm up the diet. Here is where herb teas and piping hot soups warm you from the inside. Never underestimate the importance of a nourishing home-made soup. Instant packet soups are **not** for you, nor are tinned soups. My grandmother taught me to make a 'health-building soup' that has become my stand-by and I have learned to make it with whatever is on hand, and actually *grow* a fascinating 'soup garden'!

Inexpensive, satisfyingly delicious, a quick and easy meal – I am never without a good pot of soup and everyone in the family benefits, even the dog who enjoys a ladle full of goodness over his bowl of food.

Basic winter soup

Here is my basic winter soup. Other ingredients can be added to ring the changes, but I urge you to learn this basic health-builder now. It's one of the greatest gifts I can give you and it will stand you, and your growing family, in good stead all the days of your lives. I make a big pot which can be stored safely in the fridge in a well-covered bowl and a few big ladles taken from this, and heated up (remember **never** in a microwave, but in a small pot on the stove), makes an instant meal. Serves eight.

1 small chicken, cut into pieces, giblets and all
2–3 large onions, peeled and chopped
6 stalks celery, leaves included, chopped
4–6 leeks, thinly sliced
4 large peeled grated carrots
2 thick slices of peeled pumpkin or hubbard squash or butternut or
2–3 peeled grated sweet potatoes
1 cup pearl barley
1 cup lentils
1 cup split peas
2 litres water or chicken stock
Sea salt and cayenne pepper to taste
Juice of 2 lemons
½ cup chopped parsley
½ cup olive oil

Other ingredients you can add: peeled grated potato, chopped tomatoes, chopped green pepper, chopped fennel bulb, grated turnips, grated radishes with a few leaves, chopped borage leaves, peeled grated parsnips, grated su-su squash, grated courgettes, haricot or butter beans or chickpeas or blackeyed peas, etc. (all soaked in hot water overnight or for at least 3 hours before cooking).

In a large heavy-bottomed pot fry the chopped onion and leeks in the oil until lightly browned. Add the chicken pieces and fry until lightly browned. Then add the grated carrots, lemon juice and celery. Stir-fry a few minutes. Then add everything else and the water or stock last. Stir well and cover and simmer gently for about an hour to 1½ hours, or until everything is tender and tasty. Just before serving taste test and add a little more salt and lemon juice if needed. Avoid adding flavour enhancers, sauces, chutneys, etc. Virtually all contain colourants and flavourants, like monosodium glutamate (MSG), and stabilisers. The chicken and the onions and the celery will give you a fabulously rich flavour anyway.

Serve piping hot in deep bowls and all that is needed is crusty bread and butter. For vegetarians leave out the chicken and add grated potato with chopped green peppers instead and stirfry these with the onions.

Grow your own soup garden

I plant an easy-to-grow array of herbs and vegetables for the soup pot at the end of every summer. I choose a place in full sun and dig in a lot of compost – about one large bucket per square metre. I sow radishes, buckwheat, celery, borage, parsley, kale, broccoli, carrots, leeks, onions, turnips and spring onions in neat rows and keep them moist and covered with a light layer of leaves or a shade cloth until they germinate. Then, as soon as they are vigorously growing, I thin out the rows and replant the thinnings in new rows so that each little plant has enough space to develop. I plant thyme, sage, winter savory and origanum between the rows and use the herbs in my soup as well.

There is so much enjoyment in planting and tending your own little patch of garden, and, by the way, with all the digging and bending it's a perfect work-out.

Herb teas

Here you can enjoy a quick warmer using your favourite herbs, and add a little grated ginger. Remember, ginger is a circulatory warmer and will give you instant warmth. My favourites still today are melissa and ginger and a touch of honey, rose geranium and cinnamon, spearmint with a cardamom pod or two, and thinly sliced ginger with honey and a squeeze of lemon. See page 15 for how to make a standard brew.

Rule number three

Wear warm clothing. Wear a good warm *vest* or T-shirt, big enough to cover everything, right next to your skin. A vest is the best winter warmer you could ever have. It's essential to maintain the body's heat and an old-fashioned vest is literally the only way you remain warm. Choose one made of cotton or fine wool, not a synthetic fibre.

Cotton or woollen socks are as important as the vest! And in the bitter winter cold use two pairs! Search out men's long socks and wear these under warm tracksuit pants, and don't forget the precious old long johns. Many a mother-to-be found the long john her lifesaver – or should I say warm saver – in the bitter winter days.

Forget looking fashionable. Go for the warm *underneath* instead! *That* is the secret of winter survival – warm underclothes!

Rule number four

For instant comfort, instant warmth, the hot-water bottle is top of the pops! *Nothing* beats it! For the ache in the shoulders, the twinge in the small of the back, the icy feet and the little gripes and pains, instant help is at hand. Snuggle up to the hot-water bottle. Be wary of the electric blanket – it's not good to put the baby into an electric field, nor is it good for you. So warm the bed instead with two hot-water bottles and for a soothing fragrance that helps you to unwind, tuck in a few sprigs of fresh lavender flowers between the bottle and the cover. The warmth releases the precious oils and the scent and envelopes you in a field of lavender!

Rule number five

At the end of the busy day a hot soak in a bath or shower will wash away the cares of the day and warm you so comfortingly you'll sleep well. Use a moisturising glycerine soap in a fragrance you love and at this stage go carefully with bubble bath and bath oils. Often your doctor will recommend you go without and just enjoy the warm water, or add your own water-softening bath vinegar that you have made using an apple cider vinegar base. But chat to your doctor first, in any case.

Apple cider bath vinegar

Press a few sprigs of lavender into a bottle of apple cider vinegar – the best here is *Lavandula intermedia* Margaret Roberts – or lemon thyme, or leaves of pennywort – *Centella asiatica*. Leave it in the sun for ten days. During that time strain out the herb and add more fresh leaves or sprigs of the same herb and repeat. Finally strain and discard the herbs and pour into a clean bottle. Add a dash or two to the bath. It will soften the water beautifully.

Rule number six

Lavishly massage the beautiful moisturising calendula skin moisturiser all over to keep dry winter skin soft and supple and elastic and smooth. I got very clever at developing and making this cream which I still use today as a winter moisturiser. Apply it to feet and legs and breasts and tummy particularly after the bath, and gently massage it in.

Calendula skin moisturiser

1 cup good aqueous cream
1 cup calendula petals (These bright yellow and orange winter annuals are the best winter skin treatment around. Grow them abundantly in your winter garden. Boiling water poured onto a big bowl full of calendula flowers and left to cool, can be strained and added to the bath, and to hair rinsing water, to soften and soothe.)
½ cup almond oil
2 teaspoons evening primrose oil (squeeze out capsules bought from the chemist)
4 teaspoons vitamin E oil

In a double boiler simmer the calendula petals and the aqueous cream for 20 minutes. Stir frequently. Strain and discard the petals. Add the rest of the ingredients to the aqueous cream and whisk everything together well. Spoon into a sterilised jar with a good screw-top lid and enjoy! It is superb – you'll never be without it and it's perfect for baby too!

Suitable herbs for pregnant women and the newborn

Many of the following herbs can be taken in the form of a herb tea. How to make a standard brew is described in the previous chapter and instructions should be followed carefully. Herb teas are health giving and they can also effectively treat a number of ailments. They are beneficial both during and after pregnancy and the herbs listed hereunder will give you some ideas to try out for yourself. First, however, a word of caution: do not overdo things by suddenly drinking vast quantities of herb teas. Tell your doctor what you intend including in your diet and why. Be absolutely sure of the identity of the plant before you use it.

Asparagus (*Asparagus officinalis*)
Wild asparagus is packed with the most minerals and vitamins, but for the city dweller it is almost impossible to find. The next best thing is fresh asparagus tips bought from your greengrocer or, if it is not in season, tinned asparagus will also do. These spears still have some of the vitamins and minerals needed for easing kidney and bladder ailments. The water in which the asparagus is boiled can be used as a tea for clearing kidneys; eat the spears too. If using tinned asparagus, the liquid can be drunk and the spears eaten.

Barley (*Hordeum pratense*)
Barley makes probably the most useful detoxifying tea known. It is a blood cleanser, a blood cooler, a healer of the internal organs (particularly the kidneys) and a remarkable corrector of kidney ailments. Alternated with asparagus tea, barley water will quickly ease any

kidney problems. It is rich in iron, in the B vitamins and in all the minerals, making it excellent for both pregnancy and post-natal diets. Make your own *barley water* as follows:

Boil two cups of barley in two *l* water. (Buy pearl barley from the supermarket.) Cover and simmer gently for approximately 40 minutes or until the grains are tender. Top up the water when necessary. Stand and cool, keeping covered. Then strain off the water and save the rice-like grains (eat them as a vegetable with a little lemon juice and chopped mint). Add freshly squeezed lemon, grape or orange juice and a touch of honey if liked to your barley water and drink at least two glasses a day.

I found plain barley water with a squeeze of lemon in it and a pinch of sea salt was a wonderfully refreshing pre-dinner drink when I was pregnant. When drunk at intervals during the hottest days of summer, I hardly felt the heat. Remember this for your baby too, because barley water is mild and bland and cleansing. My own children grew up on it and I am sure that this had something to do with their strong bones and perfect teeth.

Basil (*Ocimum basilicum*)

Four basil leaves in one cup of boiling water, sipped frequently, will do much to relieve morning sickness, nausea, vomiting and headaches. Chew a small leaf to help indigestion. Add a little basil to the daily salad – it has a tonic and carminative effect. A tip is to steep the flower whorls in salad oil and in salad vinegar to give the full taste and benefit of this remarkable herb.

Borage (*Borago officinalis*)

This is a wonderful, strengthening herb. It helps the kidneys manufacture cortisone by stimulating the adrenal cortex. Chopped fresh borage (ten m*l*) can be eaten daily to help constipation as it is mildly laxative. It will also greatly increase the milk flow for breastfeeding mums. A standard brew borage tea makes an excellent tonic all through your pregnancy and will keep the digestion smooth.

Sweet basil

28

Bulbinella (*Bulbine frutescens*)
This common juicy rockery plant, known as bulbinella or burn jelly plant, *katstert* or bulbine, contains an incredibly soothing jelly that will quickly heal cuts, bites, grazes, scrapes, burns, sunburn, rashes, stings, blisters, fever blisters or cold sores. It makes an excellent pot plant, too – all it requires is sunlight. Keep it growing near at hand for those everyday domestic mishaps. Simply split a leaf, split it open and rub on the soothing jelly. Apply frequently until the area is soothed. This is the best 'first aid' plant I know and children quickly get to know it and use it.

Cabbage (*Brassica oleracea*)
Warmed cabbage leaves for engorged, painful breasts are an ancient treatment, and in some country hospitals they are still used today in the maternity ward. Wear them inside your brassiere. Cabbage leaves ease milk flow, clear obstructions and keep the ducts open. This remedy works quickly and comfortingly. Warm the leaves in hot water, dry in a soft towel, and tuck into the bra.

Bulbinella

Caraway (*Carum carvi*)
A tea made from one teaspoon of seeds in one cup of boiling water is an excellent digestive. You can also add two teaspoons of caraway tea at a time to your baby's fruit juice for colic. It expels wind in both you and your baby, and it tones the liver and sweetens the bowels. If you give a teaspoon of caraway tea to your baby before meals, you will find he has hardly any wind or colic. If you suffer from heartburn, chew a few seeds or sip caraway tea, particularly if the meal has been heavy and you are feeling uncomfortable.

Chopped fresh caraway leaves are delicious in salads. If you have a patch of garden or a window-box, caraway is easy to grow.

Carrots (*Daucus carota*)
Surprisingly, carrots are very important to both the antenatal and post-natal diet as well as in your baby's diet, which is why I make a special note of it here. Carrot juice, freshly extracted in a food processor, is a remarkable 'wonder food'. Half a cup every day will do much to prevent anaemia and jaundice. Mothers who eat raw grated carrots daily and drink carrot juice throughout their pregnancies hardly ever have jaundice in their newborn babies. Carrots are good for kidney and bladder ailments, muscle tone, building up resistance to infection, worms, varicose veins and improving eyesight.

Our grandmothers actually taught us this! Invest in a juice extractor and give yourself a boost.

Catnip (*Nepeta cataria* and *Nepeta mussinii*)
This is a calming herb. Make a standard brew tea to soothe hiccoughs, heartburn, anxiety and tension in both you and your baby. As it is a refrigerant herb, it calms and cools and can be given to fretful and bedwetting children. Drink it as a nightcap too for pain relief, spasms in colic, and jangled nerves.

For baby, one teaspoon before, during and after meals will ease colic. The same standard brew will also help regulate menstruation.

Cayenne pepper (*Capsicum annuum*)
Use cayenne pepper in cooking, but not only as a condiment. It is an antispasmodic and also brings down a fever. It can help to expel worms and is a harmless and effective intestinal cleanser. A pinch of cayenne sprinkled into a little hot water will help ease heartburn. Sip it slowly.

In fact, cayenne should ideally replace black and white pepper in the diet anyway, specially if you're pregnant!

Cayenne

Celery (*Apium graveolens*)
Fresh and green, chopped into the daily salad, celery is an important blood and kidney cleansing herb. It is also excellent if you are anaemic. A standard brew tea will bring down high blood pressure, steady the nerves (and, incidentally, improve eyesight). Use the seeds as a flavouring and include stems and leaves in soups, salads and stews.

Chamomile (*Anthemis recutita*)
Probably the most loved calming herb for babies – and for insomnia in adults! Chamomile is tonic and soothing and is recognised by the medical profession as a treatment for nervous, highly strung children. A standard brew tea is a good night-time drink for expectant mothers. It will help increase milk flow and induce a good night's sleep once the baby is there. For children, use diluted with warm water and sweeten with honey. For babies, give one teaspoon at a time of the standard brew frequently to calm them down.

Comfrey (*Symphytum officinalis*)
Comfrey, also known as knitbone comfrey, is an amazing herb. Best used for skin poultices and in skin creams and healing creams, I still find it extremely helpful during a bout of bronchitis in cleaning up the chest. Make a comfrey tea with a quarter cup fresh leaf in one cup of boiling water, stand for five minutes only and then strain. Take two cups a day for three to four days, then stop immediately as soon as you feel better. For strains and sprains, warmed comfrey leaves are soothing and relaxing.

Comfrey has had a lot of controversy around it, and now doctors are advising not to take it internally, but in the case of a broken bone when healing is slow, never forget comfrey is a cell proliferator, and I have a file of cases that have the most positive views on the wonders of comfrey. For external use in creams, lotions and poultices, comfrey is completely safe, but rather do not take over a prolonged period in internal teas for chronic ailments.

Coriander (*Coriandrum sativum*)
Coriander is an easy-to-grow herb and very attractive in all forms. The seeds and/or the leaves can be made into a tea (standard brew) to ease indigestion, nausea, flatulence and – for baby – colic. This brew is also a heart and stomach tonic and traditionally the remedy was used through the ages to 'ease the pain of childbirth'.

Coriander

For colicky babies, give one to two teaspoons coriander tea before meals and one teaspoon after meals. Pour one cup boiling water over one dessert spoon coriander seeds. Stand for five minutes and then strain. Include a leaf or two in a daily salad to help indigestion. The following magical digestive medicine can be kept in the medicine chest and used by the whole family: Mix half a cup crushed coriander seeds (roughly crush them in a pestle and mortar) into half a cup honey. Place in a bottle and keep well sealed. Gently chew two m*l* of this mixture just before a meal or directly after a rich meal. Alternatively, mix one teaspoon of the mixture into one cup of boiling water. Stir well and sip slowly. For fretfulness or colic, give your baby a teaspoon just before bedtime – it may ensure a peaceful night!

Dandelion (*Taraxacum officinalis*)
Dandelion leaves, far from being just a common garden weed, are filled with vitamins and minerals and they are so full of goodness that I include them here for both mother and child. Dandelion is blood cleansing, a blood tonic, an energiser, a muscle toner, and is superb for strengthening the walls of the arteries and veins. If it is included regularly in the diet, it will strengthen tooth enamel, so remember to give it to your children. It is also excellent for the treatment of jaundice and will aid diabetes and curb over-sleepiness. Try growing this common weed in a pot, ready for picking, at your kitchen door. Add fresh leaves to the salad.

Dill (*Antheum graveolens*)
Probably the best-known carminative for babies, dill is an ingredient in the famous gripe water we all know so well. It brings up wind and it is also rich in vitamins and minerals. For relief of indigestion and flatulence, make your own dill water.

Dill water
In a screw-top bottle put 2 tablespoons dill seeds (and a fresh leaf if you have one). Pour over 1 cup of boiling water and add 1 cup of apple cider vinegar and add 1 tablespoon of honey. Shake well and keep in the fridge.

Every time you need dill water, warm a little before dosing the baby. Give one to two teaspoons before meals, and one teaspoon after meals. Another teaspoon in the middle of the night will calm a fretting baby.

Add dill leaves and a few seeds to salads, stews and soups, if you have digestive upsets. This will reduce the likelihood of colic in your baby if you are breastfeeding and you will find your milk flow will increase. A standard brew tea of dill leaves and flowers is very soothing last thing at night; it will warm and relax you.

Elder (*Sambucus nigra*)
Elder flower tea (standard brew) makes a wonderful skin and hair treatment all through your pregnancy. A stronger brew – two cups of flowers to two *l* boiling water – can be used in your bath and as a rinse for face and hair.

Elder

Ripe elderberries, pounded in honey and cooked for five minutes, make a soothing treatment for coughs and sore throats. Boil up one cup of elderberries with a quarter cup water and half cup honey.

Fennel (*Foeniculum officinale*)
Fennel makes another wonderfully soothing tea, particularly effective for water retention. The leaves in the daily salad will relieve constipation and cramps. Fennel is another herb that aids the digestion and soothes colic and flatulence. Make a standard brew and give your baby five m*l* before a meal; it will help her digest it more easily. During pregnancy, chew a few fennel seeds to ease heartburn.

Fenugreek (*Trigonella foenum-graecum*)
The seed is the important part of this easily grown annual. It can be made into a rich, strength-giving tea, full of minerals, and will give tone and vitality to the muscles during pregnancy. It will also increase the flow of milk for breastfeeding mums. Take only one teaspoon seeds and pour over one cup boiling water. Stand and steep.

Add honey and lemon juice to taste, if desired. Drink when pleasantly warm. The tea can also be taken to bring down a fever as it is cooling and soothing – sip a quarter cup at a time.

Feverfew (*Chrysanthemum parthenium*)
Feverfew is a traditional 'woman's herb'. A standard brew tea of this herb is said to help prevent a miscarriage, to help in a difficult labour and in the retention of the afterbirth. Feverfew is also both tonic and refreshing, but it is also extremely bitter, so sweeten with honey and add lemon juice. It will soothe a tension headache – eat a leaf with bread and butter. A poultice made from the crushed, pulped herb will do much to relieve painful piles.

Feverfew

Ginger (*Zingiber officinale*)
The properties of ginger are stimulating, warming, digestive and energising. Thinly slice a piece of fresh root (to equal less than a quarter of a cup), pour boiling water over it, and stand for three minutes. As a drink it will greatly relieve nausea and morning sickness, indigestion, diarrhoea and headaches. It will also stimulate the menstrual cycle after childbirth and will combat exhaustion before and following the birth.

Ginger root

If you are travelling somewhere when pregnant, take along some glacéed or candied ginger and nibble it to soothe nausea. A pinch of powdered ginger added to a cup of hot water is soothing too. The same brew will also ease labour pains.

Ground ivy (*Glechoma hederacea*)
This is a fragrant creeping hot-house plant, often grown in hanging baskets. It is a general tonic when made into a tea (standard brew) and it is used for retention of the afterbirth. As a tonic take half a cup three times a day; for retention of afterbirth, the dose is one cup every two hours.

Hollyhock (*Althaea rosea*)
A standard brew tea made from hollyhock leaves will ease inflammation of the uterus, threatened miscarriage and vaginitis. The Bedouins apparently warm the leaves in wine and give them to expectant mothers to ward off a threatened miscarriage.

Any leftover tea can be added to the bath to soothe inflamed skin, fever or the rash on a baby's bottom. The cooled tea can also be dabbed directly onto a rash or sunburn.

Honeysuckle

Honeysuckle (*Lonicera* species)
Honeysuckle tea (standard brew, using the flowers only) is a wonderful pick-me-up for those baby blues. Take a cup a day to lift depression.

Lavender (*Lavandula intermedia* Margaret Roberts)
Lavender tea is especially soothing. It will ease headaches, nausea and vomiting, so use it if you suffer from morning sickness. It makes a refreshing mouthwash too, and can also be added to the bathwater. Try fresh lavender leaves and flowers tied in a facecloth or bath glove and use as a scrub for a relaxing, deeply cleansing bath when those trying early days with your newborn are getting you down. For a fretful, crying baby a teaspoon or two of lavender tea will help to soothe and calm. Note that this is the only lavender that can be taken as a tea or used in cooking.

Lavender

Lemon (*Citrus limonum*)
Lemons are useful for bringing down fevers, cleansing the blood and soothing diarrhoea. As a tonic tea first thing in the morning for pregnant women one squeezed half of a medium-sized lemon in one cup of hot water will set you up for the day. The same tea, sipped hot or cold, will quickly relieve morning sickness or nausea. I found that even sucking a piece of lemon rind helped quell my morning sickness.

Use the squeezed lemon for a quick beauty treatment on heels, elbows and nails. Dig the nails into it; massage heels and elbows with it.

Lucerne (*Medicago sativa*)

Lucerne

Also known as alfalfa, this is a most nourishing plant as it is rich in essential vitamins and minerals and is strengthening and alkalising to the whole system. Lucerne can be sprouted and eaten in salads, but it is also an easy plant to grow in the garden. I cut my plants back frequently to ensure a crop of young shoots which I then add to salads, soups and stews, or make into teas. Lucerne is excellent for bladder and kidney ailments and for muscle tone and strength. If you take a cup of alfalfa tea daily in the last few weeks before your baby is due, this will improve your chances of an easy labour as your muscles will be well toned and strong. It's delicious cold and the leaves fresh and unwilted are excellent in salads.

Maidenhair fern (*Adiantum capillus-venenis*)

Maidenhair fern is a well-known hair tonic. Boil up three cups of water with one cup of maidenhair fern leaves for fifteen minutes. Use as a rinse to put shine and condition back into lifeless hair after the birth of your baby. It will also stimulate hair growth. A standard brew tea is good for chest colds, coughs and loosening a tight chest.

Marjoram (*Origanum vulgare*)

This is a digestive herb. A standard brew tea will soothe an acid stomach, morning sickness, nerves and fear. In nervous children it will also help to dispel nightmares and prevent bedwetting (combine with catnip for the latter). Fresh marjoram as a flavouring for savoury dishes eliminates the need for salt and pepper. Warmed marjoram placed behind a baby's ears will soothe earache. Warm a few sprigs in hot water, pat dry and hold behind the ear.

Mealie (*Zea mays*)
The humble mealie should be an essential part of our diet. The porridge is energy building and green mealies help build strong muscles and nerves. Strip young raw mealies off their cobs and toss them in a salad. The silk found in the husk is a safe treatment for kidney and bladder ailments; it will also help prevent bedwetting in children. Use some chopped raw silk in salads or make a standard brew tea. Drink half a cup three times a day or, for babies, give two teaspoons twice a day.

Melissa (Lemon balm, *Melissa officinalis*)
A much-loved, calming herb, Melissa is good for exhaustion, anxiety, nightmares, fears and nervousness. It is safe for children and extremely effective. It will quickly calm and soothe a restless baby: give two teaspoons of standard brew every half an hour. It will also stimulate expulsion of the afterbirth or delayed menstruation after the birth. It will bring down a fever and soothe gripes, colic and uterine disorders. Fresh leaves can be chopped up and included in salads. Tie a bunch of leaves in a muslin bag and put in the bath to calm hyperactive children. Also mix half a cup of melissa tea to half a cup apple juice as a cooldrink for overactive excitable children.

Mint (*Mentha* species)
Mint quells stomach pains and gas. It is a digestive aid as it combats acidity and heartburn. Chew a mint leaf for immediate relief if heartburn is a problem in your pregnancy. A standard brew tea will settle nausea and morning sickness and will also ease suppressed urine and menstruation. For a bad headache, soak a few slices of raw potato in a strong mint tea, then apply them to the forehead, holding them in place with a cloth which has been wrung out in the tea.

Diarrhoea, vomiting, gastritis and dysentery all respond to mint tea. There are many varieties, but peppermint is probably the best known and the most used. Peppermint tea makes an excellent nightcap for tired or depressed mums. It will also ease constipation and painful menstruation.

Peppermint

Nettle (*Urtica dioica*)
There are few plants that contain as much in the way of minerals, vitamins and chlorophyll as the nettle. The formic acid on the nettle's fine hairs is responsible for its sting – so wear gloves when you pick the leaves. Nettle spinach or nettle soup is surprisingly delicious and can do much to tone and strengthen the blood vessels, expel mucus from the body and combat anaemia. Nettle also aids expulsion of kidney stones. As a standard brew tea it will act as a tonic, keeping you fit and free from infection. Should you be stung by the nettle apply Bulbinella juice to soothe it.

Oats (*Avena sativum*)
Oats should form an important part of the diet during pregnancy and after the birth of the baby. It is, in fact, one food that can be taken when nothing else can be tolerated. It is a nerve and blood tonic and will help build strong teeth, hair and nails. It is rich in the B vitamins, low in starch and high in mineral content. It is also an effective anti-depressant: if you suffer from the post-natal blues, use oat straw in a tea, sipped with honey. Alternatively, eat as a porridge with milk and honey, or uncooked in muesli with fresh fruit and yoghurt. Look for the non-instant oats (avoid all instant foods during pregnancy) in health food shops and in some supermarkets. Oat straw, which is the ripened stem and leaves and the seeds, is high in calcium and builds the bones. A cup of oat-straw tea, made as a standard brew, three times a week is a super tonic.

Parsley

Parsley (*Petroselinum crispum*)
Parsley tea has a beneficial effect on the urinary system and is an excellent treatment for kidney and bladder complaints. Warmed, bruised leaves packed into the brassiere will ease swollen, painful breasts. When trying to wean your baby, this will also help dry up your milk. Use a quarter cup of fresh parsley and stalks in one cup boiling water. Stand for five minutes and strain. Take one, two or even three cups daily to dry up the milk after weaning.

Periwinkle (*Vinca major*)
Make a standard brew tea and take a quarter cup three times a day, sweetened with honey, for calming the nerves. Use the tips of the trailing stems and leaves. Use the rest of the tea, warmed, as a compress around the breasts to help dry up excess milk and excessive dripping from the nipples. Leave on for an hour. Repeat three to four times during the day.

Pennywort (*Centella asiatica*)
A fabulous herb for circulation, skin disorders, nervousness and stress. It promotes mental calm and has antiseptic diuretic digestive and anti-inflammatory properties and is superb as a tea for eczema, psoriasis and dermatitis. The juice of the leaf stops allergic skin reactions and

Periwinkle

soothes heat rash and nappy rashes and sores on babies.
  Make into a soothing lotion:
  Boil one cup of pennywort leaves in two cups of water for ten minutes. Cool, strain and use frequently as a lotion. Alternatively, simmer one cup of pennywort leaves in one cup of aqueous cream over a double boiler for twenty minutes. Then strain and use as a soothing cream for heat rash.

Pineapple (*Ananas comosus*)
Pineapple is filled with vitamins and minerals and fresh slices of pineapple should be part of your diet throughout pregnancy. Pineapple juice is also an excellent diuretic and helps ease water retention. It will help bring down urine after the birth of the baby. Eat three or four slices fresh twice a day to act as a diuretic.

Plantain (*Plantago major*)
This common weed has soothing qualities. A standard brew tea can be used as an external poultice for piles (haemorrhoids). Alternatively, crush the leaves and apply directly to the area. It can also be used for rashes, stings and bites.

Raspberry

Raspberry (*Rubus idaeus*)

Traditionally considered to prevent miscarriage and to tone the muscles, raspberry is a safe, effective herb for pregnant women. A standard brew tea, taken up to three times throughout the day, is pleasant and refreshing and works deeply within the muscles and uterus. Sweeten with honey if desired.

Try to use fresh raspberry leaves; they grow easily in South Africa. 'Autumn Bliss' is a good variety. They multiply by suckers and two or three plants will produce a good crop of leaves. Once you have them in your garden, they will be there to stay. The leaf contains an active principle called fragrine, which acts particularly on the female reproductive organs, the muscles of the pelvis and uterus. As a tea it is an excellent tonic throughout pregnancy and during labour, and will also help bring down the afterbirth. Raspberry leaf tea will bring relief from morning sickness. It can be used to treat diarrhoea and dysentery and bring down a fever in a small baby. It will also strengthen a prolapsed uterus. As a pick-me-up after the birth of your baby drink raspberry tea to combat anaemia, fatigue and lack of energy. It will also put some colour back into your cheeks, so indulge in the fruit whenever you can! It's high in vitamins and minerals!

Rose (*Rosa* species)

Rose petals are both soothing and calming, and the essential oil of roses has been used for hundreds of years as a heart and brain tonic, as well as a tonic for the uterus and ovaries. The petals can be used to make a tea (standard brew), syrup or jam to calm the nerves. (I use the deeply scented red rose 'Crimson Glory'.) The tea is also beneficial for a threatened miscarriage and for strengthening the heart before the birth of the baby. Rose petals in the bath or eaten in a salad are not only good for the skin, but are gently astringent too. Try pounding one cup of honey and a cup of petals together. Spread a little of the mixture on a slice of bread or take approximately two or three teaspoons in hot water every now and then.

Rosemary (*Rosmarinus officinalis*)
Rosemary is a remarkable herb: it is used to treat high blood pressure, heart ailments, headaches, threatened miscarriage and nervous ailments. Used externally, rosemary tea will revitalise and stimulate dull hair after your baby is born, and will also check falling, damaged hair. If you are tired and listless, a standard brew tea is wonderful first thing in the morning. A small sprig can be added to a pot of Rooibos tea and sipped as a pick-me-up during the day.

Sage (*Salvia officinalis*)
A much-loved herb, sage is probably known best for its soothing properties in treating coughs, colds and fevers. The standard brew tea, however, is also good for nervousness, digestive discomfort, flatulence and constipation. It may have the effect of reducing milk flow in nursing mothers.

Sage

Salad burnet (*Sanguisorba officinalis*)
This is a tonic herb and, as a tea, will cleanse blood disorders and skin problems. Use as a wash on the skin or add to the bathwater. It is soothing and gentle for sunburnt skin and can be used as a wash for baby's eczema or nappy rash.

Southernwood (*Artemisia abrotanum*)
This is a renowned 'female' herb and is excellent for treating bladder or kidney problems: make a standard brew and take half a cup morning and evening. It also makes a good wash and lotion for baby's rashes and scalp infections: use half a cup.

Strawberry (*Fragaria vesca*)
Strawberries are an excellent treatment for blood disorders and the fruit is excellent for anaemia, lowered vitality and as a nerve tonic. When the fruit is not in season, a standard brew tea of the leaves can be used for bowel disorders, fevers, irregular menstruation and to prevent miscarriage. It will also clear liver disorders and excessive perspiration. Externally, it can be used on the skin for rashes and eczema, and as a lotion for sore eyes and styes.

Thyme (*Thymus vulgaris, T. serpyllum*)
These thymes and the lemon flavoured thyme (*Thymus citriodorus*) are natural antiseptics. Thyme soothes indigestion, flatulence, nervousness, liver ailments, headaches and even nightmares. It helps expel the afterbirth and is excellent in the treatment of an inflamed or diseased uterus. It can also give relief in cases of engorged breasts – used either as a tea or as a poultice.

Vine. Also known as grapevine (*Vitis vinifera*) Vine leaves, tendrils and grapes are so beneficial to all-round health that for expectant mothers they act as a tonic for the whole system. Young leaves and tendrils can be made into a health-giving tea (standard brew) to bring down a fever, relieve constipation, lift depression and tone the blood. Chop a few tendrils into salads and use the leaves in cooking.

Vine

Watercress (*Nasturtium officinale*)
Watercress is an effective treatment for blood disorders. For mothers having difficulty breastfeeding, it will increase the milk flow; chop up half a cup of watercress, and steep in a cup of slightly warmed milk. Allow the milk to cool and, when cold, drink the liquid (eat the watercress afterwards). You will find that your milk flow increases quickly. Watercress also helps ease a stiff back and stiff joints, particularly useful towards the end of your term. It is such a wonderfully tonic herb, a little watercress in the daily salad is beneficial to the whole system.

Yarrow (*Achillea millefolium*)
A warmed yarrow leaf compress will soothe painful haemorrhoids, nose bleeds and earache. Apply externally. Note: Use only the common pink and white flowered yarrow – this is the true medicinal yarrow. When young, the flowers are pink, and they lighten and whiten as the flower ages.

Yarrow

42

reparing for the birth

Pamper yourself in the last month before your baby is born. It is the last chance in a long while you will get to do so. These last few weeks are most important for both you and your baby. Try to enjoy each day and live every moment to the full. Life will never be the same again!

Keep an eye on the following checklist:

- *Sleep.* Be sure to get as much as you can. Rest in the afternoons if at all possible. If you have other children, try to farm them out to friends for a couple of hours. Read and relax all you can. Go to bed early. You need to build up strength for the sleepless days and nights ahead.

- *Avoid watching TV.* Television 'rays' are still an unknown quantity. Tests are being done but no one is yet quite sure of the effect they have on human life. Avoid, therefore, exposing your unborn child to any rays, X-rays, laser beams, microwaves, computer rays, electric blankets, etc.

- *Fluids.* In this last month fluid intake is tremendously important. Drink fresh fruit juice, plenty of water, and calming herb teas. Increase your intake of fresh milk.

- *Diet.* What you eat in these vital weeks is of utmost importance. Your baby is big now and he or she will be needing extra food in preparation for entering into the world. Increase your intake of vitamins E and C. Pantothenic acid found in the B vitamins taken just before the birth helps combat stress. Make sure to eat plain yoghurt daily, and lots of green leafy vegetables, in the last week especially, to provide vitamin K (which prevents haemorrhaging).

Step up calcium intake: remember that dolomite and magnesium phosphate act as a natural painkiller and may be helpful if you are in any discomfort. In general try to eat only whole foods and avoid junk foods or drinks during this period.

- *Exercise.* Step up your exercise routine to keep your body tuned and supple in preparation for labour. Do exercises every day under the supervision of, or taking the advice of, your physiotherapist or antenatal instructor. Walk somewhere every day, even if it is only to the corner shop.
- *Nipple treatment.* Massage cream into your nipples to strengthen them before your baby begins breastfeeding. Cracked nipples is a common but avoidable problem when you first start feeding and, if left untreated, can be very sore indeed.
- *Stretchmark massage.* As the baby grows very quickly in this last month, do not neglect this important task.
- *Be happy.* Read, listen to peaceful music, avoid all stressful people, places and occasions if you possibly can.
- *Deep breathing.* Concentrate on your breathing exercises; allow them to become automatic to you. You will probably be feeling fairly uncomfortable now and anxious for the baby to be born.
- *Case packed.* Don't be caught unawares – have your case ready at least six weeks before you are due. Prepare the baby's room a month in advance, and anything else in the home that needs doing, so that this last month is a holiday.

A day or two before you are due, wash your hair, do your nails and have a friend give your feet a pedicure and massage – you will not be able to reach them, and you won't have time once the baby is there. Above all, be happy. You are about to become a mother!

he newborn

The first few weeks after your baby is born can be a confusing, often exhausting time, especially for first-time mothers. Above all try to relax until you find your routine. An unstressed mother goes a long way to making an unstressed baby. Now is the time when you will lay the foundation for your relationship with your new son or daughter. It is the time for bonding and nurturing, for intimacy and loving closeness.

Breastfeeding

This is the greatest gift you can give to your child. The sucking reflex in a newborn baby is very strong and the infant should be put to the breast as soon as possible. The first 'food' your baby will get from sucking is called 'colostrum'. This watery substance is rich in protein and will prevent him or her falling prey to infection in these first few days. While sucking is instinctive and comforting to your baby, it also stimulates the breasts into releasing the milk.

If you have looked after yourself throughout your pregnancy, you should have no difficulty breastfeeding. Do not worry that your baby is not getting enough milk. Every baby's needs are different and you will find what suits your child best as the weeks go by. You will learn to recognise a 'hungry' cry and will probably have a more contented baby if you 'demand feed'. In other words, do not try to stick to a rigid four-hourly schedule. If your baby seems hungry every two or three hours, go ahead and feed. You will soon settle into a routine.

45

Breastfeeding is the easiest and best way of feeding your baby: he or she gets the perfectly balanced food served at the perfect temperature. It is the opportunity for him to get to know your smell and your touch and respond to them as to no other. Breastfeeding bonds you and your baby for all time.

Your diet while breastfeeding

Make sure that you keep up your fluid intake – fresh milk, water, bland fruit juices (avoid undiluted orange juice for a few weeks) and herb teas. You will need now to add more Brewer's yeast to your diet; the powdered form is excellent. Increase your intake of liver, wheatgerm, kelp and take extra protein. Keep up your vitamins. Keep a 'nibble-bowl' handy and fill it with raisins, almonds and sunflower seeds.

The following is an energy-giving recipe for mums who are breastfeeding.

Nursing mother's energiser

2 cups whole milk
½ cup non-instant powdered milk
3 teaspoons debittered Brewer's yeast (Mega yeast is easily available.)
3 teaspoons sunflower oil
1 cup mashed fruit (e.g. banana, grapes, peach, pawpaw)
1 egg
3 bonemeal or dolomite tablets, crushed
2 teaspoons fresh mint, chopped (melissa is also excellent)
3 teaspoons lecithin granules

Whirl all ingredients in a blender. Add another cup milk. Drink ½ – ¾ cup at intervals throughout the day (you should have finished it by bedtime). Increase yeast after a week or two up to 4 teaspoons.

Herbs to help milk flow

Borage, dill, fenugreek, raspberry and periwinkle are all good for keeping up your milk flow. The last mentioned will also help dry up dripping breasts. Lettuce cooked in milk will increase milk flow and also help you sleep: Boil up one chopped lettuce in one *l* milk (use the dark outer leaves as well). Simmer for five minutes with the lid half on. Drain and use the milk as a drink, storing excess in the fridge to add to soup. Eat the leaves with a little chopped celery and thyme as a vegetable. It is surprisingly delicious.

Cracked nipples/Engorged breasts

If you have taken proper care to harden your nipples during your pregnancy in preparation for breastfeeding, cracked nipples should not be a problem. If you feel a sharp, shooting pain in your nipple when the baby is feeding, it is probably a cracked nipple. This is a painful condition and should be treated quickly. Immediately stop feeding on that side and express your milk manually or with a breast pump. Do not be tempted to put on baby oil; rather use a vitamin E and comfrey cream. Make sure that you wash well before nursing again.

Parsley packed into the brassiere or warmed cabbage leaves will ease a blocked duct or painful, engorged breasts. Thyme works well this way too, as does the inner side of a pawpaw skin.

For how long should you breastfeed?

You should try to breastfeed for at least three months to give your baby a good start in building up resistance to infection and getting the quality and quantity of nourishment needed. If it is possible to continue for longer, then do keep it up for as long as your baby wants to. Your baby will indicate when he or she is losing interest in the breast (probably round about eight to nine months).

My first two children were big babies and needed extra food by six months. I started then to supplement their diets with cow's milk and solids. The youngest one was content to nurse until she was eight months old.

Nurse no longer than one year of age. After that you're not helping the child grow into independence and you're not doing him or her a favour.

47

Formula feeding

If you are unable to breastfeed for any reason, you can prepare your own bottle feeds. Never allow a small baby to feed on his or her own propped up on a pillow. Firstly, it is dangerous – a baby can easily choke. Secondly, your baby needs to be cuddled and held and talked to while feeding. The following milk formula is safe after six months. It is an old-fashioned one and I have used it most successfully. If you are bottlefeeding earlier, take the advice of your doctor or clinic sister before giving this formula.

Start by adding one-third boiled cow's milk to two-thirds boiled water for one week. Increase to half boiled water and half boiled milk the second week. In the third week mix two-thirds milk to one-third water and finally go on to full strength cow's milk by the fourth week. Pour the formula into sterilised bottles and keep in the fridge. I found this an excellent way of adding more substance to feeds and eventually replaced the midday breastfeed with this bottle. Let the baby take all she needs and do not force her.

Sterilising

Once you switch to formula or supplementary feeding, you will need to sterilise bottles, teats and formula. The easiest way of doing this is to make up the day's formula early by filling three, four or five bottles, covering with teats and placing them all in a steamer or large pot with a rack on which they can stand, and covering with a lid. The boiling water and steam sterilise the bottles and no valuable protein is lost in the process.

Keep the bottles in the fridge and, when required, take a bottle and stand it in a jug of hot water until it is the required temperature (lukewarm). Never use a microwave to heat up bottles.

Remember that babies get thirsty as well as hungry. A sterilised bottle with plain boiled water in it should always be on hand. Should you have a colicky baby, add a little herb tea (standard brew) to the water: mint, melissa, dill, fennel and caraway are all perfectly safe and very soothing. Usually three teaspoons to half the bottle of water is a good quantity to add.

The older baby

As your baby grows older he or she will require more fluids. Fruit juices, freshly squeezed and diluted, can now be added to the diet. Add a little mint or catnip tea if the fruit is a little acid. If you think it may be too sour, put in two to five m*l* honey. Beware of adding sweeteners to your child's diet as this early stage. Try not to encourage a sweet tooth. The only acceptable sweetener is honey, and then it must be used very sparingly.

Introducing solids

Once your baby has indicated that breast or formula feeds no longer satisfy his or her hunger completely, it is time to introduce solids. Some babies require solids sooner that others, but milk feeds should be enough until your baby is three months old. Be guided by your doctor or clinic sister.

The first and easiest solid should be in the form of porridge at breakfast time. Oatmeal porridge is a nourishing starter. Do not use instant oats; find the real, large-flake kind obtainable from health food shops and some supermarkets. Make it rather runny and press it through a sieve with a wooden spoon, or liquidise it. Mix in a little boiled milk or plain yoghurt and a touch of honey. Mealie-meal porridge is also full of goodness and can be alternated with oats.

Steamed vegetables and fruit

You will soon find your baby is ready for a good lunch. Invest in a steamer if you do not already have one. Boiling vegetables and fruit reduces their nutritional value and allows precious vitamins and minerals to escape. A steamer, particularly one with two or three layers, works well and allows you to do both fruit and veggies at the same time.

Suitable vegetables to start off with are: gem squash, courgettes, peas, green beans, green mealies, carrots, pumpkin, beetroot, cabbage, spinach, lettuce, cauliflower, broccoli, sweet potatoes and potatoes. All of these can be steamed – lettuce too – and then put through a liquidiser with a little of the water, or pressed through a sieve with a wooden spoon.

Serve plain vegetables to start with, and introduce one different flavour at a time. Give your baby three or four teaspoons for lunch and gradually increase the amount to two or three tablespoons. He will also let you know when he has had enough. As your baby gets used to new tastes and textures, add in some chicken jelly, or the water in which chicken was boiled. Try putting in half a teaspoon of Marmite; some babies enjoy the change of taste and the saltiness.

Suitable fruits to start off with are apples, peaches and pears. These three are the most suitable for steaming. Pawpaw, grapes (peeled and pipped), mangoes and overripe bananas can also be given early on, but are best served raw, mashed and sieved.

Always introduce one new taste at a time to see if your baby likes it; he will let you know in no uncertain terms if he doesn't! Resist sweetening food with sugar; always try to keep food as natural as possible. Add a little plain yoghurt by way of a change, or some chunky cottage cheese.

Protein

Meat, chicken and fish are the best sources of protein and can be gradually added to the diet after three months. Prepare by steaming or boiling as this is the most easily digestible method for the baby.

Boiled chicken

Place one chicken piece (e.g. breast) in a pot with enough water to cover. Add a stick of celery, one thumb-length sprig of thyme, a peeled sliced carrot, a squeeze of lemon juice and one teaspoon of sea salt. Cover and simmer for approximately an hour or until chicken is tender.

Drain and save the water and keep it in a sealed container in the fridge. Mix a spoon or two of this 'jelly' (it will set once in the fridge) with the baby's vegetables. Finely mince some of the chicken breast and mix it in with the vegetables. Offer a teaspoon at a time at the midday meal.

Beef or liver stew

Place diced beef or liver in a pot, add water and add a squeeze of lemon juice, a pinch or two of sea salt, a sprig of marjoram or fennel, one diced carrot and a small stick of celery. Boil up in enough water to just cover the chopped pieces. Mince finely when tender and add a teaspoon or two to baby's vegetables, with some of the water in which it was cooked.

Steamed fish

Place a piece of deboned hake in a steamer. Squeeze over it a little lemon juice and two tablespoons of plain yoghurt. Add a pinch of sea salt. Steam until tender. Flake the fish and mix in with the baby's vegetables (just two to three teaspoons to start with). Spoon over a little yoghurt sauce. Never fry fish for a baby as it is very indigestible done this way. Fish is an important source of phosphorus and iodine and should be included in the diet at least once a week.

Basic menu up to six months

Milk is still the major item in the baby's diet up to six months. If your baby is also on solids, she should be getting porridge (oats or mealie-meal) in the morning, with a little plain yoghurt or milk added, and steamed fruit and vegetables, and protein from chicken, meat and fish at midday.

In the beginning, as you start off on solids, give your baby milk first, then top up with solids. Later, once your baby is used to new tastes and textures, start the meal with solids and top up with milk.

It is a good idea to keep a notebook on your baby's early eating patterns so that anything that may cause a rash or diarrhoea can be identified quickly and eliminated from the diet.

From six months to one year

Gradually introduce your baby to egg yolk (discard the white) by lightly boiling an egg, and mixing it into porridge, a teaspoon of yolk at a time. You can also make a simple custard, using milk and egg and a touch of honey.

Custard

1½ cups milk
1–2 teaspoons honey
2 egg yolks, beaten (discard the whites)

Bring the milk and honey to the boil in a double boiler, or on a very low heat. Add the egg yolks and keep stirring (it curdles easily – if it does, liquidise it), allowing it to thicken gently. If you want a thicker custard, stir 2 teaspoons of Maizena (corn starch) into a little cold milk and add to the mixture.

If you leave out the honey, you can add a little of this custard to minced fish or chicken, or to mashed potatoes.

Curd cheese

This is full of nutrition and can be added to porridge, vegetables or fruit. As you will still be pureeing everything in a liquidiser or through a sieve, it will enrich whatever it is added to and the baby will accept the taste.

> 2 cups milk
> 1 sprig melissa or lemon thyme
>
> Place the herb in the milk and allow to stand overnight out of the fridge, keeping the container covered. Next day, when it is thick and sour, discard the herbs, and pour through a muslin cloth to let the whey drip out.

Use the curd in mashed banana, sparingly to start with. My babies all loved it! Cover and keep the excess in the fridge.

Ripe bananas

Only very ripe bananas should be used. Choose the brown, blotchy skinned ones that are soft to the touch. Mash well and add a little first to the porridge. Once the baby gets used to the taste, mash the banana on its own with a little home-made custard.

Avocado

Mashed avocado is very easy to digest and rich in vitamins and minerals. Choose a ripe soft avocado and mash it well. Add a little to mashed potato to start the new taste off. Most babies love the taste of avocado.

Oranges

Choose very sweet ones, squeeze out the juice and add it to herb teas (e.g. melissa, standard brew), or peel and put them through a liquidiser and add to mashed pawpaw or banana. Go cautiously with oranges, as many babies find them too sour and too sharply acidic. Two teaspoons added to half a cup of melissa tea is the best way to start.

Yoghurt

Yoghurt is more easily digested than milk, but be sure to use only plain yoghurt, never the coloured fruit ones. Always remember, should your baby ever have to take an antibiotic, to include lots of yoghurt in the diet.

Sprouts

Mung beans and alfalfa seed can be sprouted easily and a few, liquidised and added to the baby's porridge or vegetables, can be introduced now. Sprouts are highly nutritious; their protein, vitamin and mineral content surpasses most other foodstuffs. They should become part of your family's daily menu and, if given now, will give your baby a taste for this health food throughout his or her life.

Raw foods

From ten months onwards your baby can safely have minced or pureed raw foods: carrots, beetroot, apple, celery, cucumber and tomato are all suitable. (Raw beetroot is excellent, but may colour your baby's stools and urine pink – do not be alarmed.)

Pulses

Peas, beans, lentils, chickpeas and soya beans all need to be soaked overnight, then slowly cooked and pureed with water. I soak mine with a sprig of thyme, marjoram or a dill leaf, then cook them with fresh marjoram or thyme, and two to three fennel or dill leaves: these are all digestive aids. Mix a little of this pureed mush into vegetables. Mix with mashed avocado and yoghurt. All three of my babies loved lentils and split peas cooked together.

Cheese

Cottage cheese is easily tolerated and can be mixed with steamed fruit. Introduce your baby to sweetmilk cheese now too by finely grating a little and stirring it into vegetables. Do not cook cheese as this makes it indigestible. Stay with only cream cheese or sweet-milk until your baby is over three years, then introduce cheddar.

Nuts and sunflower seeds

Almonds or pecan nuts can be minced with sunflower seeds into a flour and added to fruit or vegetable dishes. Rich in protein and minerals, they are important in the baby's diet. Never give your baby peanuts or cashew or macadamia nuts. These three nuts can be the cause of severe allergies and intolerance.

Carob

Chocolate is not suitable for babies (or for you!). Rather use carob from the carob pod, which is a more natural flavouring and contains vitamins A, D and B, riboflavin and niacin – all important for glowing health. Carob can be bought at a health shop.

Points to remember

- *Sweetening* A sweet tooth is cultivated – not inherited! Keep sweetening to a minimum, and use only honey as an additive. Never give sweets as a reward. Modern society is addicted to sweets. Beware!
- *Colourants* These can cause allergies, so try to avoid them wherever possible. Read up on every item you buy. Stay with the fruit and vegetable naturals.
- *Preservatives* Read the ingredients on every package you buy. Get to know what unnatural substances are in prepared foods and avoid them.
- Feed your baby only the best fresh, natural, uncontaminated food. Prepare it as naturally as possible, and as your child grows older feed him or her as much raw food as possible. Grow your own, if at all feasible, and support organic farmers.
- Read up on health and nutrition; there are any number of books on the subject available from your local library.

- Avoid fast foods, junk foods, sweets, crisps, ice cream and refined foods. There are a vast number of substitutes for snack foods that are tasty and nutritious, like raisins, dried fruit and sunflower seeds (and natural popcorn, no syrup or salt, for the older child).
- Keep up intake of natural vitamins for both your baby and yourself.

Teething and finger foods

After your baby has cut his first teeth, he will start putting everything into his mouth. Now is the time to provide chewable foods that will aid tooth formation and soothe gums.

Biltong

A thick finger of biltong, long enough for your baby to hold onto with his whole hand, is an excellent teething food. Choose a lean piece, not too spicy.

Rusks

These can give your baby lots of chewing fun. Make your own, cutting them large enough for your baby to handle without choking:

10 slices home-made wholewheat bread (about 2 cm thick)
³/₄ cup hot water into which 3 teaspoons of yeast extract (e.g. Marmite) has been dissolved.

Cut the slices into fingers and, using a pastry brush, brush the yeast extract and water onto all sides of the bread. Space a little apart on a wire cake cooler and bake at 120 °C for about 1½ hours until crisp and dry. Cool and store in a tin.

Teething biscuits

½ cup wholewheat flour
½ cup soy flour
3 teaspoons soft honey

1 egg yolk
4 teaspoons sunflower oil
2 teaspoons mint or thyme, chopped finely
enough milk to make a stiff dough

Mix all ingredients together, slowly adding the milk last of all. Pinch off pieces of dough and roll into a 2 cm thick sausage about 8 cm long. Place on a floured baking tray. Bake at 180 °C for about 20 minutes. When cool, store in an airtight tin.

Chopped foods

Gradually get your baby used to chopped or roughly mashed foods rather than purées. This will help with chewing which is good for teething too. Mix grated raw carrot or chopped tomatoes into mashed food. Set out trays of *finger foods* for your child to try. These are important in the baby's diet and, as she is intrigued by different objects now and will pick up and put different things into her mouth, she will enjoy this activity. She will also search out the things that her system needs. Finger foods will teach independence too and will get your children interested in food.

Set out manageable pieces of any of the following on a plate or tray, but never leave a baby to eat on her own in case she chokes. Let your baby experiment without you hovering, but keep an eye on her.

Hardboiled egg, sliced; tomato wedges; green peas, cooked; cucumber slices; celery stick; banana; pear; carrot sticks; cubes of cheese; raisins; wholewheat bread made into tiny sandwiches with cottage cheese; small pieces of *deboned* cooked fish, chicken or meat, or a small pile of cooked minced meat; a few grapes, peeled and seeded; piece of peach, peeled; small pile of chopped sprouts.

Basic menu for twelve months and upwards

Your baby is now becoming a child. He is probably starting to take his first shaky steps and 'talking' to you non-stop. He is doubtless displaying a mind of his own too and, hopefully, if you have taken care over his diet, he is happy, healthy and sturdy. You can now broaden the diet considerably.

Breakfast

- Porridge, yoghurt (plain), little honey to sweeten
- Boiled or scrambled egg
- Wholewheat toast with yeast extract (e.g. Marmite) or touch of honey
- Mug of milk to drink
- Piece of fruit (e.g. pawpaw, peach etc.)

Mid-morning

- Fresh fruit juice with herb tea
- Rusk or biscuit

Lunch

- Steamed vegetables, meat, fish or chicken
- Salad finger foods
- Fresh fruit, custard
- Mug of milk

Afternoon snack

- Fresh fruit juice, fruit pieces, biltong

Supper

- Soup, wholewheat bread, sandwich or savoury dish
- Fruit (e.g. banana mashed with yoghurt or cottage cheese)
- Mug of milk

Remember to season food with herbs rather than salt and pepper. A little coarse sea salt is acceptable.

$\mathcal{F}$ood for healthy kids

Remember that the correct, healthy way of eating learned as a baby will become a way of life as your children grow up. It will give them pride in their bodies and the way they look. Self-esteem and a feeling of self-worth are important fundamentals for a happy life. The following are a few recipes my own children have thrived on and enjoyed. Develop your own variations as you go along, and change them around to encourage an interest in mealtimes.

Breakfast stand-by

In a thermos flask the night before, pour in ½ cup oats that have been mixed with 1 cup hot water. Add 1 tablespoon seedless raisins, 1 tablespoon almond meal ground in a coffee grinder, 1 tablespoon sunflower seeds and 1 tablespoon wheatgerm. Shake up well and seal.

Next morning the mixture will be fluffy and swollen. Serve with a little warm milk and yoghurt and a touch of honey. My children grew to love this porridge, particularly on a winter morning, as it set them up for the day. They still enjoy it today!

Homemade yoghurt

Yoghurt, plain and unsweetened, is easy to make. It is a superb health food, and easily assimilated by the body. As all the family benefit from yoghurt, a good quantity should always be at hand. (I use it in baking as well as in porridge or muesli, and in sauces.)

2 cups whole milk
2 tablespoons natural yoghurt

3 tablespoons skim milk powder

Bring the milk to the boil and simmer for four or five minutes. Allow to cool to 43 °C, i.e. pleasantly warm. Mix the yoghurt and milk powder and pour in a little of the boiled milk, stirring well. Add the rest of the milk, stirring continually. If you have a yoghurt maker, pour the mixture into it; if you don't, pour it into a wide-necked thermos flask. The secret is to leave it undisturbed for about five hours or until it is set. (If you leave it in the thermos for too long it will taste too acid.) Once it is set – between five and eight hours – place in the fridge and use as required.

Yoghurt recipes

Instead of adding milk, cream or custard to fruit or porridge, use plain yoghurt. The following flavourings will be great favourites with your baby as well as older children.

Sweet puddings

- *Pureed fruit* (e.g. apples, strawberries, pawpaw, mango, peaches, bananas). Add a pinch of cinnamon and a little honey. Whirl in some plain yoghurt and serve as a dessert.
- Soak *dried peaches or apple rings* in water overnight. Chop or mince and add to yoghurt. Toss in a few chopped dates if you like.
- Put a tablespoon each of *almonds and sunflower seeds* through a wheatmill or coffee grinder. Mix into 125 ml yoghurt and add a touch of honey or molasses.

Savoury

Liquidise a *peeled tomato* with two *cucumber* slices (also peeled) into 1 tablespoon yoghurt.
- Add 2 tablespoons finely chopped or minced raw *carrots, celery and lettuce* to 1 tablespoon yoghurt. Mix well and serve as a vegetable.
- Add a little grated *sweetmilk cheese* and a little finely minced celery or spinach to yoghurt.

Banana oats

This is a delicious breakfast dish. The whole family will love it.

1 tablespoon large-flake, non-instant oats (for baby, mill them)
³/₄ cup milk
½ ripe banana, mashed
½ cup plain yoghurt

Cook oats gently in the milk, and blend in banana and yoghurt. Stir well into oats and cook one minute more. Serve with a touch of honey.

Health soup

Serves six.

³/₄ cup barley, soaked overnight in water
³/₄ cup haricot, kidney or butter beans, soaked overnight in water
2 stalks celery, chopped
1 onion, chopped
2–3 tomatoes, skinned and chopped
2 carrots, grated
1 cup chopped spinach or cabbage
1 cup chopped greens (e.g. borage, dandelion, comfrey etc.)
sea salt
thyme or marjoram (about 3 sprigs stripped off the stalks)
juice of 1 lemon
oil
2 l water or stock

Brown the onions and the celery in a little oil. Add all the other ingredients, cover and simmer until the beans and barley are tender. Adjust seasoning to taste. Liquidise a portion for the baby and serve with fingers of buttered wholewheat toast. He will enjoy dipping the toast into the bowl. Soon he will enjoy the soup served unliquidised as he sees how the rest of the family eat it.

Vary this soup by adding a chicken carcass or soup bones, or stir in a cup or two of yoghurt. Use whatever vegetables are in season – courgettes, leeks, kohlrabi, cauliflower, broccoli and pumpkin all make delicious variations.

Cold soup

Serves six.

1 cup chopped celery
2 tomatoes, skinned and chopped
1 small lettuce, chopped
1 small cucumber, chopped (about 1 cup)
2 carrots, grated
1–2 ml chopped greens (e.g. spinach, dandelion leaves, beetroot leaves,
*   borage etc.)*
1 cup cooked beans, lentils or peas
thyme or marjoram sprigs (about 2 of each stripped)
sea salt
lemon juice to taste – usually the juice of 1 lemon
3 cups water or stock
1–2 cups plain yoghurt

Whirl all ingredients in a liquidiser. Sprinkle with parsley and serve. This is a health- and energy-giving soup on a hot day and very refreshing for a baby who does not feel like eating. You can also add any of the following: cooked brown rice, fresh courgettes, watercress, beetroot, apple, pineapple, grapes, almonds, or finely minced cooked chicken or fish.

Savoury mince

This is an excellent stand-by and, with vegetables added, makes a nourishing dish for either lunch or supper.

1 kg lean mince
1 onion, finely chopped
2–3 medium tomatoes, skinned and chopped
1 cup chopped celery
2 teaspoons fresh thyme, marjoram, sage or basil, chopped
2 carrots, grated
little oil
pinch of sea salt
fresh parsley, chopped
water or ½ cup yoghurt, mixed with water

Fry the onion in the oil until lightly browned. Add the mince and brown slightly. Add celery and tomatoes and stir in well. Then add the salt, herbs, carrots and honey, and the yoghurt. Add enough water to make it fairly soft and liquid and cook slowly until done, stirring occasionally and adding more water if necessary. Strain off some of the gravy to add to a small baby's vegetables as it is full of nourishment.

Serve with mashed potato and gem squash and mashed green beans for a substantial midday meal. Alternatively, add a spoonful to scrambled eggs for supper, or mix with a little brown rice and stuff into lettuce leaf 'boats' or celery stick 'canoes'.

Chicken

Boil, stew or roast chicken and serve thin pieces that can be well mashed. Save the water if you boil it to make a nourishing gravy. This can be used as a consommé or chilled soup on hot summer evenings on its own. The water sets into a tasty jelly which can be used in vegetables, other soups or as a savoury jelly for a hot day. When you boil up a chicken add celery sticks, diced carrots and onion slices.

Fish

Select unsmoked, unsalted, bland white fish (e.g. hake). Always steam or poach it rather than fry it. Serve with vegetables and savoury white sauce.

Pulses (dried beans, peas, lentils etc.)

Soak all pulses overnight in water. Next morning, boil in enough water to cover. Toss in a sprig of thyme, marjoram or a piece of celery. Boil until tender in a covered pot, then drain, mash and add to soups, stews or vegetable dishes.

Cook one cup lentils and one cup split peas together until tender. Mash and flavour with salt and lemon juice.

Mixed with mashed avocado and yoghurt, it makes a delicious dip or salad. This is an important food containing vitamins and minerals and can be added to any savoury dish. Serve with a little finely chopped fennel or caraway seeds to ease flatulence.

Humus

This is a Middle Eastern favourite food and is delicious added to vegetables or spread on thin biscuits or bread.

1 cup chickpeas, soaked overnight
2 teaspoons chopped thyme
juice of one lemon
2 tablespoons chopped parsley
sea salt to taste
4 tablespoons plain yoghurt
4 tablespoons sunflower oil
2 teaspoons fresh marjoram or 2 teaspoons chopped fresh mint

Cook the chickpeas with the thyme until tender. Drain and liquidise, adding yoghurt and other ingredients until a thick paste is achieved. Store in jars in the fridge.

Grains and nuts

Brown rice, barley, whole or crushed wheat and mealie-meal are all excellent foods, some at least of which should be included daily in the diet. Grains can be boiled in water and the water used for stock.

Barley stirfry

1 cup barley
1 l water
sunflower oil
1 onion, chopped
1 tomato, skinned and chopped
2 courgettes, thinly sliced
2 teaspoons fresh thyme, chopped
sea salt

Boil barley in the water for half to three-quarters of an hour or until tender. Strain. Save the barley water for drinks. In a pan, heat a little oil, add onion and the barley grains. Add tomato and courgettes.

Stirfry, adding a touch of sea salt and the thyme (mint or fennel are also suitable). Stir well with a wooden spoon. Add a little water if it gets too dry and a teaspoon of yeast extract (like Marmite). This makes a delicious supper dish.

Potato nests

6 medium potatoes
½ cup milk
2 tablespoons plain yoghurt
1 tablespoon chopped parsley

Boil potatoes in their jackets, then peel and mash. Mix in milk, yoghurt, a pinch of sea salt, and the parsley. Shape into nests in an ovenproof dish.

Filling
½ cup cream cheese
1 egg
2 tablespoons wheatgerm
2–4 tablespoons sprouts

Mix ingredients and scoop into the nests. Place under the grill for 5–10 minutes or until slightly firm. Serve with a slice of tomato, carrot sticks etc.

Cold fillings: any of these will make a delicious light meal: grated cheese, tomatoes, cold cooked peas, finely chopped lettuce, celery, grated apple, or mix a few together like cheese, celery and tomato, peas and lettuce and apple, etc.

Pulse sausage

2 cups cooked dried beans, peas or lentils
1 egg, well beaten
½ cup wheatgerm
4 tablespoons grated cheese
1 teaspoon Marmite
chopped parsley, thyme or mint
few breadcrumbs

Mix all ingredients except breadcrumbs. Shape into sausages and roll in the crumbs. Fry gently in a little hot oil or place in an ovenproof dish, dot with butter, pour in a little oil and bake for 15–20 minutes at 180 °C. As a variation, add cooked minced meat or minced cooked chicken. Children of all ages *love* this dish!

Cheese and rice bake

1 cup brown rice, cooked
3 eggs, separated
1 cup milk
1 cup grated cheese, mild
2 tablespoons wheatgerm
2 tablespoons lemon balm mint, mixed with thyme and finely chopped

Whisk eggs and milk. Stir cheese, wheatgerm and herbs into rice. Pour into a shallow baking dish. Bake at 180 °C for 20–30 minutes or until golden and set.

Dips

Small children love to dip and lick. Try offering them dips of mashed avocado with a little lemon juice, or cottage cheese mixed with a little yoghurt and chopped herbs (e.g. borage flowers, nasturtium flowers, celery leaves, mint, parsley etc.). Arrange a tray of some of the following to go with the dips: strips of carrot, celery sticks, sugar-snap peas, small tomatoes, slices of cucumber, pineapple fingers, apple slices, etc.

Cakes, biscuits, breads

There is nothing quite like home-baked bread fresh from the oven. It is not difficult and can be a labour of love for your growing family. Remember though:
- Use only wholewheat flour or brown flour
- Use only butter
- Substitute honey or molasses for sugar or icing sugar
- Avoid all sticky, sugary recipes. Seek out alternatives.

Fruit bars

1 cup stoned dates
1 cup dried apricots, soaked overnight in water
1 cup dried figs, soaked overnight in water
$\frac{1}{2}$ cup sultanas
$\frac{1}{2}$ cup sesame seeds or coconut
$\frac{3}{4}$ cup almonds or pecan nuts
little honey to bind ingredients if necessary

Finely mince all ingredients, mix together and press into a greased tin. Leave to harden for about 6 hours. Cut into squares or bars. Roll in coconut if it feels too sticky.

Fruit bread

1 tablespoon butter
1 cup wholewheat flour
1 cup brown bread flour
3 teaspoons baking powder
$\frac{1}{2}$ teaspoon sea salt
$1\frac{1}{2}$ cups milk
1 tablespoon runny honey
2 tablespoons treacolin or molasses
$\frac{1}{2}$ cup seedless raisins

Grease and line two small loaf tins (or 4 to 6 miniature tins, or 1 large tin). Mix dry ingredients. Gently warm milk, treacolin, honey and butter, add raisins and stand for 5 minutes. Add to the flour mixture. Mix well and pour into tins and bake for 20 minutes at 180 °C (a little longer if using a larger tin). Serve buttered slices for a delicious teatime snack.

Quick health bread

Get into the habit of baking your own bread. No bought bread can substitute for your own freshly baked loaf. This is my standard easy bread. I bake a loaf every day and it takes only 10 minutes to make.

500 g Nuttywheat
2 teaspoons dried yeast
1 tablespoon cooking oil
1 heaped tablespoon crushed wheat
1 heaped tablespoon sunflower seeds
1 heaped tablespoon sesame seeds
1 heaped tablespoon oats
1 teaspoon sea salt
2 teaspoons brown sugar
½ cup raisins or sultanas
warm water 350 mℓ

Mix the yeast with the sugar, oil and warm water. Add all the other ingredients except the crushed wheat. Grease a loaf tin. Spoon the mixture into the tin, sprinkle with crushed wheat, cover and set in a warm place, Allow the dough to rise level with the top of the tin (it takes about half an hour). Then bake in a hot oven (180 °C) for 40 minutes.

(If you like, sprinkle a little crushed wheat into the greased tin before you put the mixture in.)

Sunflower seed sweets

1 cup sunflower seeds, finely ground
½ cup ground almonds
½ cup finely minced prunes and dates
fresh orange juice (usually about ½ a cup)

Combine seeds and almonds. Mix in prune and date mixture. Add enough orange juice to make a paste. Pinch off balls and flatten them. (Toss them in coconut if you like.) Place on a baking sheet and bake at 200 °C for 2 hours or until they are slightly crisp.

Halva

1 cup sesame seeds
1 cup sunflower seeds
enough honey to make a stiff dough

Grind the seeds together in a coffee grinder or a spice mill and add enough honey to bind. Spread into a greased container and keep in the fridge. Slice off squares or roll small balls in coconut. Keep in the fridge and wrap each little ball separately in greaseproof paper if you're going on a hike – for energy.

Health ice cream

½ cup fresh cream
½ cup nut cream (see following recipe)
¼ cup honey
1 cup grape juice

Blend fresh cream and nut cream. Add rest of ingredients. Pour into ice-cube tray and, when almost frozen, stick a toothpick or ice-cream stick into each cube. As a variation, try adding half a cup mashed strawberries, peaches or raspberries.

Nut cream

½ cup almonds or pecan nuts, crushed and ground
1 cup water
about 2 teaspoons honey to taste

Blend nuts and water to a smooth paste. Add honey. Store in the fridge. Add to ice-cream, drinks, mix into yoghurt, custards etc.

Drinks

There are any number of variations in drinks for children. Fresh fruit juices are the healthiest and can be added to yoghurt, barley water, milkshakes and herb teas. I never put away my liquidiser while my children were small and, as they grew older, they learned to make their own milk- or fruit-shakes whenever they needed a drink. Try different blends, using melissa or mint herb teas as a base (standard brew). Add fruit, almonds, egg yolk, dried fruit that has been soaked and softened in water, barley water or a little carob powder. Experiment and have fun – healthy fun.

Fresh fruit juice

Nothing can replace the nutritious and delicious benefit of fresh fruit juice. Invest in a juice extractor if possible and squeeze your own. Orange, pawpaw, pineapple and guava juice are only a few of the many fresh juices you can try.

Chocolate fruit shake

Blend a banana into 1 cup fresh milk. Add 1 teaspoon carob powder and beat until foamy. Serve chilled.

Vitality shake

Whisk 1 tablespoon nut milk and 1 egg yolk into 1 cup cold milk for a deliciously different milkshake. Add a little honey if you like and 1 teaspoon of wheatgerm to make it extra healthy.

Almond drink

Almonds and pecan nuts are suitable for children; avoid peanuts, Brazil nuts and pistachios until they are much older.

1 cup milk
1 tablespoon ground almonds
1 tablespoon ground sunflower seeds
2 teaspoons honey OR 1 teaspoon molasses

Whirl all ingredients in a liquidiser. Add half a ripe banana or half a ripe peach or 4 or 5 strawberries. It is the nicest milkshake ever!

Herb ice cubes

When making ice cubes, place a couple of mint leaves, violets or borage flowers into the tray. Serve with fresh fruit juices.

$\mathcal{T}$reating common childhood ailments

Biochemic Tissue Salts

There are twelve remarkable minerals that are commonly known as Tissue Salts. An eminent German physician, Dr Schuessler, discovered on analysis that when the human cell is reduced to ashes it exhibits twelve minerals. When any of these minerals are lacking we show signs of distress, illness and emotional stresses.

The Tissue Salts are present in our food when it is grown in mineral-rich, well-worked and naturally composted soils, but today's chemical fertilisers and fumigants have leached the soil, and therefore our foods, of these precious life-building minerals.

Dr Schuessler (1828–1898) developed these mineral salts into easy-to-take little pillules or tablets. One sucked under the tongue is the child's dose, or it can be crushed into a teaspoon of warm water, or your pharmacy will order the Tissue Salts in drop form from Natura Homeopathic Laboratory in Pretoria, who manufactures them. The drops are especially easy for babies – a dosage of five to ten drops in a little water or in the feed, or milk.

Their names go alphabetically with corresponding numbers:

No. 1 is Calc. Fluor.   No. 7 is Kali. Sulph.
No. 2 is Calc. Phos.   No. 8 is Mag. Phos.
No. 3 is Calc. Sulph.   No. 9 is Nat. Mur.
No. 4 is Ferrum Phos.   No. 10 is Nat. Phos.
No. 5 is Kali. Mur.   No. 11 is Nat. Sulph.
No. 6 is Kali. Phos.   No. 12 is Silicia

For more information, refer to *Tissue Salts for Healthy Living*.

Children respond quickly to the Tissue Salts, and I will be forever grateful for the comfort and safety that these incredibly effective little tablets gave me as a young mother on a distant farm. Many a situation and many a drama were solved with Tissue Salts and soothing herb teas. The bathroom cupboard was lined with Tissue Salts and they quickly learned to find the correct one. Anyone waking in the night with a sore throat would grab No. 4 or for a sore ear No. 1, No. 3 and No. 4, for a headache No. 2, and a nightmare No. 2 and No. 6. No one could overdose, and every child obligingly opened a little mouth and his or her dog opened his little snout, and the sick bantam opened his little beak, and so I could go down the row, dosing everyone, with quickly gratifying results.

One of my most amazing experiences has been with our new little baby Samantha who, when only a few weeks old, showed the worrying symptoms of projectile vomiting. Nothing could be kept down, my daughter-in-law could not produce enough milk with endless sicking up and the little baby was not putting on weight. The doctors suggested performing a small operation on the stomach valve which put me into a terrible anxiety as I knew this procedure *could* cause later effects like chronic heartburn and flatulence and so on. So we all immediately turned to Tissue Salts with my daughter-in-law taking several so that the baby could get enough with her milk. One tablet of No. 8 – Mag. Phos. – was dissolved in one teaspoon of warm water and given to Samantha just before her feed. Miraculously it stayed down, and a second tablet of Mag. Phos. was crushed in a teaspoon of warm water and given to her directly after the meal, and the happy little baby (who only two hours before had drawn her tiny knees up onto her tummy and cried with such distress) lay kicking and smiling peacefully in her pram. And she has never needed to take Mag. Phos. again! Mag. Phos. is the most incredible anti-spasmodic for cramps and colic and for projectile vomiting – it's pure MAGIC!

For a few ideas on how effective the Tissue Salts are, read through this list. One tablet sucked or crushed (or five drops in a teaspoon of water) is the first dose, and then another ten to twenty minutes later in a crisis situation until the problem returns to normal:

- to encourage the closing of the fontanelle, No. 2 and No. 12
- for colic, No. 2 and No. 8
- constipation, No. 4
- cradle cap, No. 5 (give a tablet three times a day and make a lotion by crushing four tablets of No. 5 in warm water and dabbing it on to soften the cradle cap.)
- for delayed dentition, No. 1 and No. 2
- for vomiting, food regurgitation, flatulence, hiccoughs and tummy ache, No. 8
- for fretfulness, No. 2
- for crusty inflamed vaccinations, No. 5
- for inflamed sore gums and mouth ulcers, No. 5; with No. 4 if the little mouth is swollen and red
- for teething, No. 4, No. 2 and No. 8, all together as often as six times a day and rub a little of the solution on the gums. I make up a little bottle with a dropper of ten drops each of No. 4, No. 2 and No. 8 with one tablespoon of water and I keep it handy for rubbing onto the hot sore little gums. When there is excessive salivation – I found my son's little bibs were absolutely soaked with dribble during his teething – No. 9 given about five times during the day eased the condition beautifully.
- tremors and convulsions, No. 1 and No. 12
- twitching limbs, No. 1 and No. 12
- vomiting undigested milk, No. 4, No. 8 and No. 10
- colds, No. 1, No. 2 and No. 4
- flu, No. 4, No. 5, No. 9, No. 11 and No. 1

NOTE: There is an easy-to-find natural remedy range called The Margaret Roberts Herbal Remedies, manufactured by Fithealth. Ask your chemist to order them for you if he doesn't have in stock.

There is a natural antibiotic, a natural laxative, a natural painkiller, natural hayfever and sinus treatment and a natural hyperactivity treatment. All are herbs finely ground in a capsule format. You can easily open the capsule and sprinkle it into a little milk or fruit juice or into the food so the baby takes it easily. Directions are on the bottle. Ask your doctor to check if it is suitable for your child's current ailment. The capsules are available only at pharmacies.

Common childhood ailments

Always work with your doctor when you have a sick child. The following are some simple tried and tested remedies for a variety of ailments commonly affecting children at one time or another. Keep your doctor informed.

Allergies

Stop all food that could possibly be causing the allergy. For two days feed the child barley water, bland vegetables (e.g. squash, pumpkin, potato, pawpaw, apple, oats). Herb teas (standard brew) will be safe too; lemon balm is the best.

Tissue Salts: No. 9, No. 7; Food allergies No. 4; Allergic rash mix ten drops of No. 9 and ten drops of No. 3 together and add three tablespoons of water. Dab onto the area.

Antibiotic

If your child has to go onto antibiotics, be sure to add extra yoghurt (plain) to the diet, as well as B vitamins. Grapes, thyme and borage will all assist the body to fight infection. Salads (liquidised with yoghurt for a baby) are important to help clean out the system; include a little lettuce, celery, parsley, fennel, cucumber and lightly cooked cabbage.

Tissue Salts: No. 4 and No. 5.

Asthma

Avoid all white foods (i.e. egg white, milk – for the time being – white sugar, white rice, white flour). Include a little comfrey in the diet and honeysuckle flowers steeped in honey as a cough mixture. A pinch of ginger sipped in melissa tea is calming and soothing; mullein tea is also beneficial. Fresh fruit and vegetables are very important in the diet too. Oats is a good asthma treatment; give as a porridge morning and evening.

Tissue Salts: No. 4, No. 6 and No. 8, also No. 1 and No. 5 when necessary.

Bed-wetting
Pick one fresh thumb-length sprig of marjoram and one of catnip.
Steep in 60 ml boiling water for three to four minutes. Sweeten with
a touch of honey. Remove herb and give this drink to your child
just before he or she goes to sleep. Start with three to four teaspoons until your child gets used to it. Chamomile tea – only half
a cup.
Tissue Salts: No. 2, No. 8 and No. 12.

Boils
A warmed poultice made from a comfrey leaf, placed over the boil,
will help to draw it to a head. Warmed pumpkin or oats are also
effective treatments.
Tissue Salts: No. 3, No. 5 and No. 12. Also make a paste of these
three Tissue Salts and apply under the poultice.

Bruises
Make a soothing poultice using comfrey leaves, marjoram, fenugreek seeds or violet leaves, warmed in hot water and applied to
the area.
Tissue Salt: No. 12.

Burns
Rub on the juice of the bulbinella, sourfig leaf or aloe vera leaf or
the inside of a banana skin. Comfrey ointment is soothing for burns
too. Alternatively, an arum lily leaf acts like oiled silk. Warm in hot
water and apply over aloe vera gel.

Calming
Melissa or chamomile tea are both soothing, as are teas (standard
brew) made from marjoram or violet flowers and leaves. Add the
cooled tea to a little juice.
Tissue Salts: No. 2, No. 6 and No. 12.

Carsickness
The day before you embark on a long car journey, make the diet
light, i.e. no fats or heavy proteins. If you are setting off in the

morning, serve a breakfast of oats porridge with a little yoghurt and fruit, before departing. Avoid giving sweets or cooldrinks during the journey. Warm melissa tea with apple juice is safe and soothing. Sucking on a wedge of lemon will help too. When the baby is old enough give him or her a mint leaf to chew. Ginger also soothes – add a pinch of bland herb tea. Try to keep a queasy child distracted and carry a facecloth, towel and water in case of accidents. If the child should be sick despite all precautions, sprinkle the car upholstery with bicarbonate of soda to remove the smell. This is one of the few times a little flat Coca-Cola helps quickly and easily. Take tiny sips.

Tissue Salts for nausea: No. 4, No. 8, No. 9 and No. 10.

Chestiness
Effective herb teas for a chesty child can be made using any of these herbs in a standard brew herb tea: comfrey, mullein, sage, violets, maidenhair fern or melissa. I often combine comfrey and maidenhair fern with sage. Add a little honey to the herb tea to sweeten, if liked.

Tissue Salts: No. 1, No. 4, No. 7 and No. 12.

Colds
Herb teas of either comfrey, sage, melissa, thyme, chamomile, elder flowers, ginger, maidenhair fern and watercress will all bring relief. Hollyhock, violets and marjoram can also be made into effective teas. Olbas, a herbal medicine, available at chemists and health stores, is worth trying too, especially for a blocked-up nose. Steam with a few drops in a bowl of boiling water with a towel tent over the head.

Tissue Salts: No. 1, No. 2 and No. 4, and later No. 5, No. 7 and No. 9.

Colic
Herb teas of any of these: catnip, chamomile, thyme, caraway, coriander, melissa, dill, fennel and mint will all soothe a colicky baby.

Tissue Salts: No. 7, No. 8, No. 9, No. 10 and No. 11. Crush one of each and mix into a little melissa tea.

Constipation
Herb teas of violet flowers, chamomile and borage (fresh only), fennel, the mints, mullein, sage, strawberry, grapes (vine leaves and tendrils too) are all good. Add a little honey.

Tissue Salts: No. 1, No. 3, No. 9, No. 11 and No. 12 and the Margaret Roberts Intestinal Cleanser capsules.

Convulsions
Herb teas of catnip, chamomile and melissa. Include celery in the diet, as well as comfrey, fenugreek, marjoram and mint.

Tissue Salts: No. 4, No. 8 and No. 11.

Coughs
Equal quantities of sage (fresh chopped leaves), honey and lemon juice mixture. Alternatively teas of thyme, honeysuckle flowers in honey, watercress, comfrey, elderberries, maidenhair fern, mullein, nettle and violet are all soothing.

Tissue Salts: Congestion: No. 4 and No. 7; Dry cough: No. 5 and No. 8; Chronic cough: No. 2, No. 4 and No. 6; Irritating cough: No. 1 and No. 5.

Cradle cap
Make a standard brew tea using rosemary or pennywort (*Centella*) and use, lukewarm, as a rinse, and dab on frequently.

Tissue Salt: No. 9.

Cramp
Herb teas of chamomile, ginger, rosemary and lavender will ease painful cramps.

Tissue Salt: No. 8.

Croup
Tea with fresh ginger and honey or chamomile tea.

Tissue Salts: No. 4, No. 5, No. 7 and No. 8.

Cuts (minor)
Wash clean with a brew of rosemary, pennywort (*Centella*), salad

burnet or lavender, then rub on bulbinella juice.

Tissue Salts: No. 3 and No. 4, and make a lotion of them – dab on frequently.

Diarrhoea

Flat Coke and cream crackers are an excellent remedy and one of the only times I will recommend a carbonated soft drink! (The other time is for travelling sickness.) For a baby, whisk out the bubbles and mash the biscuits into the Coke to make it easier to take. Ginger tea is also effective. Include grated apple, raspberry leaf tea and mint in the diet.

Tissue Salts: No. 3, No. 4, No. 8, No. 10 and No. 12. If it is bad smelling add No. 6; thin and watery add No. 9 and No. 11; yellow add No. 7 and No. 11.

Earache

Try Olbas, available from health shops and some pharmacies. It is a remarkable patent medicine for a number of ailments. Dab it behind the ear to soothe the pain. Do not, however, put it into the ear or nose. Mullein, marjoram and nettle leaves, crushed with hot water and made into poultice, can be held in place behind the ear.

Tissue Salts: No. 2, No. 3, No. 4 and No. 11, and No. 7 if the ears are blocked.

Eczema

As a wash use a tea made from either elder flowers, penny-wort (*Centella*), nettle, salad burnet, strawberry or oats (applied externally).

Tissue Salts: itching and weeping No. 9; chronic No. 3, No. 5 and No. 9; general eczema No. 3, No. 6, No. 7, No. 10 and No. 11.

Fatigue

Raspberry leaf tea, ginger tea and rosemary tea will put more energy into a listless tired child.

Tissue Salts: No. 1, No. 2, No. 9, No. 10 and No. 12.

Fever
To bring down a persistent fever, try the following in the diet: borage, catnip tea, strawberries, mint tea, raspberry leaf tea, celery, lemon, melissa tea, parsley (fresh), sage tea and grapes (including vine leaves and tendrils). Frequent sips of herb teas or cool water will help too. Use these herbs in a bath of tepid water: raspberry leaf and mint. Pour boiling water over one cup of each. Stand and cool. Strain and add to bath.
Tissue Salts: No. 4 and No. 9 frequently until the fever breaks.

Flatulence
Asparagus, catnip, caraway, the mints, thyme, dill, basil, coriander, fennel, marjoram and melissa are all safe and effective. Chew a piece or make a tea.
Tissue Salts: No. 2, No. 5, No. 6 and No. 8.

Flu
Encourage lots of water and diluted fruit juices and chicken soup in the diet. Tea made from comfrey, mullein, sage or violets will help fight flu. Drink lots of barley water.
Tissue Salts: No. 1, No. 4, No. 5, No. 9 and No. 11. Take one of each eight times through the day.

Fretting
Soothing herbs for a fretful child are teas of either chamomile, melissa, thyme, dill, catnip, lavender or violets. Include oats in the diet.
Tissue Salts: No.2 and No. 8.

Grazes
Aloe vera, bulbinella, yarrow, plantain and rosemary will all soothe a grazed knee. Dab on or make into a standard brew tea and use as a wash.
Tissue Salts: No. 3 and No. 4. Make into a lotion and wash out the cut.

Haemorrhoids

Comfrey, yarrow, feverfew, oats and plantain are good for this painful problem. Use as a poultice or as a brew for a wash.

Tissue Salts: No. 1, No. 4 and No. 12. Also make into a lotion. Add No. 5, No. 7 and No. 9 if there is itching and burning.

Hayfever

Eat a little honeycomb every day, chewing the wax for a few minutes. Mullein and violets in a tea are also effective.

Tissue Salts: No. 6 and No. 9.

Headache

A tea of either rosemary, violets, melissa, lavender, thyme, basil, catnip and ginger will soothe an aching head. Make standard brew teas and include in the diet. Give a little frequently.

Tissue Salts: No. 6, No. 8 and No. 9.

Heartburn/Indigestion

A tea of either fennel, caraway, the mints, melissa and sage will bring relief from the discomfort. Chew a leaf or make into a tea. Chew a few caraway seeds.

Tissue Salts: No. 2, No. 8 and No. 10.

Hiccoughs

Try catnip tea or a teaspoon or two of peppermint tea. One teaspoon of honey in a little warm water also helps. A couple of drops of Rescue Remedy (available from health stores) will work wonders.

Tissue Salts: No. 1, No. 5 and No. 8.

Infections

Asparagus, barley, carrot and lemon in the diet will help fight infection. In the form of a tea take ground ivy, thyme, sage or pennywort (*Centella*).

Tissue Salts: No. 4 and No. 5.

Inflammation
This can effectively be treated with any of the following teas: rosemary, thyme, pennywort (*Centella*), borage, comfrey and sage. Include barley, lemon and basil in the diet.
    Tissue Salts: No. 4, No. 5 and No. 7.

Insect bites and stings
Rub on juice of bulbinella leaves or aloe vera. A poultice made from borage, comfrey, sourfig, mint or plantain leaves will bring relief. For a bee sting, first remove the sting and then apply the inside of a banana skin to the painful area. For a wasp sting, dab vinegar onto the sting for instant relief.
    Tissue Salts: No. 3, No. 8, No. 9 and No. 10. Suck a tablet of each. Make into a paste as well and apply to the area.

Insect repellent
Place bowls of any of these herbs in the baby's room to keep insects at bay: the mints, pennyroyal, sweet basil, caraway, feverfew, southernwood, sage, lavender.

Jaundice
Include in the diet: asparagus, barley, carrot, dandelion and oats.
    Tissue Salts: No. 3, No. 5, No. 10 and No. 11. Take one of each at least four times a day.

Kidney and bladder ailments
In the diet include asparagus, celery, parsley, ginger, pineapple, barley, carrot and mealies which will assist in clearing these conditions. Make a tea of lucerne with nettle, violets and a little comfrey and give half a cup frequently to flush the kidneys. Also give as much water as the child can take.
    Tissue Salts: No. 3, No. 4, No. 6 and No. 10.

Nappy rash
A lotion made from either elder, salad burnet or pennywort (*Centella*), are all gentle and safe for a baby. If the rash is bad, try to leave the baby's nappy off for a while each day. Lay your baby on a

folded nappy on an old blanket while you keep an eye on him or her. Comfrey cream, applied daily, will keep your baby clear of rash. See page 86 for the recipe.

Tissue Salts: Nappy rash tissue salt has been known through the decades as No. 3. I made it into a lotion and added it to baby's bath. Tissue Salts No. 3, No. 5, No. 6 and No. 9 can also be made into a lotion, as well as taken per mouth.

Nausea

The following herbs have a soothing effect on a queasy stomach: melissa, the mints, ginger and dill. Make any of these herbs into a tea and add a squeeze of lemon juice.

Tissue Salts: No. 4, No. 8 (especially for violent nausea), No. 9 and No. 10. For nausea due to overindulgence, take No. 5 and No. 11.

Nervousness

To calm a nervous or highly strung child, include the following either in the diet or as standard brew teas: melissa, rose petals, thyme, chamomile, elder flowers, lavender, sage, violets and violet leaves. Add mealies, oats, celery, strawberries to the diet and barley and barley water.

Tissue Salts: No. 2, No. 6 and No. 8.

Nosebleed

Yarrow or mullein: make a poultice of the leaves and hold against the nose until bleeding stops.

Tissue Salts: No. 4 and No. 9.

Pain

Any of these herbs will bring relief: catnip, Californian poppy, coriander, feverfew, ginger, melissa, the mints. Make into a tea.

Tissue Salts: No. 2, No. 8 and No. 12.

Rash

Children are prone to sudden, sometimes inexplicable, rashes. Treatment with one of these herbs is soothing and effective: juice from sourfig, bulbinella, strawberry or aloe vera.

Tissue Salts: No. 3, No. 5, No. 6, No. 7, No. 9 and No. 11. Make into a paste and apply as well as taking by mouth.

Sedative
Herbs which can calm a nervous or hysterical child, with no harmful effects, are: melissa, catnip, ginger, elder flowers or chamomile, made as a tea, and give oats porridge for supper.
Tissue Salts: No. 2, No. 3 and No. 6, or all the phosphates No. 2, No. 4, No. 6, No. 8 and No. 10.

Sinus
The mints, pennyroyal, Olbas (available from health stores) or lavender will ease this uncomfortable affliction. Simply bruise the herb and inhale, or inhale the steam from pouring boiling water over the herb under a towel tent, and add a few drops of Olbas.
Tissue Salts: No. 2, No. 3, No. 5, No. 7 and No. 9.

Skin disorders
Include the following in the diet: elder flowers, marjoram, salad burnet, watercress, apples, lucerne, carrots, parsley, fennel, celery and rose petals. Use the following externally: pennywort (*Centella*), aloe vera and bulbinella.
Tissue Salts: No. 1, No. 3, No. 7, No. 9 and No. 11.

Sleep
Sleep-inducing, soothing herbs are: chamomile, melissa, catnip, lavender and rose. Take in the form of a nightcap tea – half a cup or even a few teaspoons.
Tissue Salts: No. 2, No. 4, No. 6, No. 8 and No. 10. Grinding teeth, No. 10.

Sore throat
Sourfig, sage and ginger will soothe a bad throat. Chew a piece of leaf, or make a tea of sage or ginger.
Tissue Salts: No. 1 and No. 4.

Sprains
Make a comfrey poultice with warmed leaves wrapped around the area and held in place with a crepe bandage.

Stomach disorders, cramps, colic, indigestion
Grated apple, chamomile and the mints or melissa teas, are all effective treatments.
    Tissue Salts: No. 3, No. 8 and No. 10.

Sunburn
Bulbinella, comfrey cream, salad burnet, waterlily stem (squeeze on the juice) will soothe effectively. Alternatively, dab milk directly onto the sore areas.
    Tissue Salts: No. 4, No. 8 and No. 9.

Swelling
Make a compress from comfrey, borage, violet or plantain leaves. Warm in hot water first. Apply directly to the area, hold in place with a crepe bandage.
    Tissue Salts: No. 4, No. 9 and No. 12.

Tearfulness
Tea of cinnamon and honey, or melissa tea.
    Tissue Salts: No. 3 and No. 9.

Teething
Dab Rescue Remedy (available from health stores) onto gums, or two to three drops into the mouth. Include dandelion leaves in the diet for strong teeth. Oats, too, will help build strong, healthy teeth.
    Tissue Salts: No. 1 and No. 2, and No. 9 to stop the dribble.

Temper tantrums
Chamomile or melissa tea.
    Tissue Salts: No. 6, No. 8, No. 9 and No. 12.

Tonic
In need of a boost after an illness, for example, include in the diet: watercress, strawberry, oats and take teas of either catnip, chamomile, rosemary, sage, salad burnet or pennywort (*Centella*).
Tissue Salt: No. 2.

Vomiting
Try Rescue Remedy (available from health stores). Melissa or the mints can be made into soothing herb teas. Sip frequently. Iced water with lemon juice is effective too.
Tissue Salts: No. 8, No. 10 and No. 11.

Warts
Dab wart frequently with fig leaf juice (the milky sap). The inside of a banana skin, taped onto the wart and exchanged for a fresh piece every day for ten days, will be effective too.
Tissue Salts: No. 1, No. 5, No. 7, No. 9 and No. 11.

Worms
Carrots and pumpkin pips will assist in expelling worms. *NB. Only use the pumpkin pip remedy from three years old and upwards.* Chew seven pumpkin pips first thing in the morning (on an empty stomach) for ten days. Peel the pip of its outer covering first. Eat the inside of the pumpkin pip. Follow with a cup of melissa tea.
Tissue Salts: No. 10 and No. 11.

Medicine chest basics

Rearing children means having always to be on one's toes! Nearly every day someone will need attention and you should be prepared as best you can. Often treatment is necessary immediately until you can get to your doctor or at least talk to him or her. Make sure, therefore, that your medicine chest is always stocked with basic essentials. Always keep it out of reach of your children.

Have the following on hand and all the Tissue Salts. My formula for crisis – No. 2, No. 6, No. 8 and No. 12 – works wonders!

- Scissors
- Tweezers
- Crepe bandages
- Gauze
- Lint
- Sticking plasters

Rescue Remedy – Dr Bach's famous drops – can be used in an emergency and many a time they have been a lifesaver for me and my family. Health stores and some pharmacists stock them. I keep them in the kitchen, in the bathroom, beside my bed, in my car. They can be used for shock caused by any trauma, e.g. fall, wound, fright, fear, burn, bite or broken limb. Just a few drops into the mouth and directly onto the affected area frequently give you the time you need to cope with the emergency and calms both you and the child.

Olbas – This is a patent herbal medicine for aches and pains, earache and blocked noses. Do not apply drops into the nose or ears; dab a little externally on the nostrils and behind the ears. It is good for insect bites, headaches and a stiff neck. Most pharmacies have it, as well as health stores.

Vitamin C – for infections, and resistance to coughs and colds, vitamin C is invaluable in the medicine chest. Take 250 mg daily, stepped up to 500 and even 1 000 mg in times of infection and illness.

Keep your home-made *comfrey cream* in the medicine chest for all those scratches and grazes, little burns and rashes.

All-purpose healing cream

½ cup chopped comfrey
½ cup chopped pennywort leaves
½ cup elder flowers or ½ cup calendula flowers

Simmer the ingredients in a double boiler in 500g of good aqueous cream for 20 minutes. Cool for 10 minutes, then strain and add 2 teaspoons vitamin E oil and 1 teaspoon tea tree oil. (Both these oils can be bought from your chemist.) Keep in a sterilised jar in the medicine chest.

Now that you have read this little book, my hope is that my experience in bringing up my own three children can be of benefit to you. Experience, after all, is an excellent teacher, and I learned more about health in rearing them on that isolated farm than I did in my hospital training.

May this little book start you and your baby on a road of glorious health and happiness. May it change your life and give you much pleasure as you watch your children grow.

For all that I have learned in the rearing of Pete, Gaily and Sandy, I must thank them for giving me such a rich, full and healthy life!

Bless all mothers – their task is a huge one, but one filled with much joy. As a parting thought I read this somewhere and loved it: 'God couldn't be everywhere, so she created mothers.'

Margaret Roberts
The Herbal Centre
De Wildt
North West Province
South Africa

ndex